Zakynthos

today and yesterday

**A complete guide for travellers
with 168 colour illustrations
and maps**

MICHALIS TOUMBIS EDITIONS S.A. - ATHENS

Texts: J. SOLMAN, D. THEODORAKATOS, AG. VISVARDIS, J. VOGIATZIS
Translation: G. COX, J. SOLMAN
Maps: NORA ANASTASOGLOY
Photographs: M. ARGYRIADOU, T. GIGANTES, M. TOUBIS

Art Work: NORA ANASTASOGLOU
Four-colour editing: YANNIS KOLLAROS
Photosetting: KIKI SANTORINAIOU
Montage: NIKOS PRASIANAKIS
Printed by: M. TOUMBIS GRAPHIC ARTS S.A., Athens - Tel. no. 9923874

Our particular thanks to
T. KONIDOU, D. VITSOS, M. ARGYRIADOU and L. MERKATI, all of Zakynthos, for the con-
tributions they have made to this book.

Among the most striking flowers in the rich flora of the countryside of Zakynthus is the
Orchis italicus, which can reach 25-30 cm in height, with its splendid inflorescence
(photograph from the collection of L. Merkati).

Fair isle, that from the fairest
of all flowers,
Thy gentlest of all gentle
names dost take!
How many memories of what
radiant hours
At sight of thee and thine
at once awake!
How many scenes of what
departed bliss!
How many visions
of a maiden that is
No more — no more upon
thy verdant slopes!
No more! alas,
that magical sad sound
Transforming all!
Thy charm shall
please no more.
They memory no more!
Accursed groud!
Henceforth. I hold thy
flower-enamelled shore,
O hyacinthine isle! O purple Zante!
Isola d'Oro! Fior di Levante!

Edgar Allan Poe

Foreword

Zakynthos, the Fioro de Levante, flower of the East; the island of song, the island of love. This place truly is magic; its gentle, calm landscape wins over the heart, as do its clean, translucent sea and its superb beaches. The verdant plains are covered with a carpet of wild flowers in spring, and the courtyards fill with jasmine. On the low hills are shady pine forests, and pretty villages which keep up the traditions of earlier days. There are natural phenomena in plenty, and places which call out to be explored, to yield their secrets to the visitor.

The beauty of Zakynthos has been praised by many, great poets and visitors, locals and visitors alike. Since early in this century, it has attracted the interest of famous scholars and travellers. In 1904, the Grand Duke Ludwing Salvator of Austria, a well-known traveller, published his two volumes entitled Zante, which gave a detailed description of the history, folklore, geography and customs of the island, accompanied by sketches and —rare for the time— photographs. On this island, nature and art come harmoniously together. This was one of the beacons of modern Greek culture: the island of Kalvos, of Solomos and of Xenopoulos, and one of the places where the graphic arts, wonderfully conjoined, reach a peak of achievement.

The islanders are cheerful, hospitable and fond of a good time, and they were responsible for creating a local culture whose features are familiar throughout Greece and far beyond. Although tourism has grown very rapidly in Zakynhtos in recent years, the islanders have stayed the same, particularly in relation to their hospitality —for which they are famous— their pleasure in life and their vitality.

We have produced this tourist guide in an attempt to give readers a fuller understanding of the history of this place, of the progress of its people through the past to the present, of the dignified town —hard tried by nature— with its sights, and of its pretty villages. But there is much, much, more which readers will discover for themselves when they go to Zakynthos. The island captivates those who visit it, exerting the same kind of irresistible charm which the lines of Andreas Kalvos express so well:

Zakynthos, beautiful and unique
Has won my heart.

Contents

Agriculture and Morphology

Zakynthos, the sixth (progressing north to south) of the Ionian islands, lies 17 nautical miles west of the Coast of Ilias (Cape Tripiti) and 14 nautical miles south of Cephalonia.

In prehistory, Zakynthos was still a part of the Mediterranian seabed. A series of quakes caused the formation of chasms and pushed up the land mass, forming the island as we know it today. Southeast of Zakynthos is an area in the sea which geologists have named the "Pit of Inoussae" where the Mediterranean has its greatest depth (5,090 metres).

These sudden geological upheavals of prehistory caused the formation of many small islets around Zakynthos, as well as many reefs and cliffs. The largest of the islands belong to the Strofades group. During this time as well, the shoreline, was broken up and beaches were formed, some in the south with sand and calm waters and others in the west, contained between high clifs and very rocky.

From the geological standpoint, the island can be divided into three sections. The first, in the west, is made up of limestone rock strata, formed 100-70 milion years ago. It is here that the constant action of the sea has caused the formation of caves and large underwater holes. The second section, in the northeast, was formed from much more recent rockbeds and is mainly of a clayish nature, which makes it very fertile. Here the rain water collecting in the porous rockbed is prevented from seeping down further by the clay, giving rise to springs and wells. Finally the third section includs Mt Scopos extends to the cape Gerakas. Much of the rock strata here is hydrated calcium sulphate. The peak of Skopos is an impressive mass of this mineral which, through tectonic pressure, was forced out to the surface, pushing aside the surrounding layers.

Some of the most significant geological phenomenon on the island are the medicinal sulphur springs around Tetartia (in the village of Yerakari), at Kolosourtis (behind Aliki), at Vromoneri, or the Waters of Kareri, Paliochora, Xyngia, as well as two springs at the port of Nafthis (or Keri). At a spot on the southwest side of the island water mixed with bitumen spurts out of the ground. Wells of bitumen have been found in

other places as well, but due to their great depth they have never been exploited, and no attempt has ever been made to drill for oil commercially.

There are a number of caves in many areas of Zakynthos (Dracospilia, Aghios Yerasimos, Haghiotis, etc) and they are very interesting to visit. The most important of these is on the seashore, and is known as 'Galazia Spilia' or the Blue Cave, although it is actually two consecutive chambers. It was discovered in 1897 at Aspros Vraxos, northeast of Cape Skinari. It gets its name from the blue hue of varying shades, caused by the refraction of light on its surface waters, which tints everything inside it.

The island has a wonderful Mediterranian climate with moderate, rainy winters and cool, dry summers. It is a climate favourable for the cultivation of delicate crops, olives, vines, garden vegetables and citrus fruits. The average temperature is 11.7 degrees centigrade in January and 27.5 degrees centigrade in August.

The humid west, northeast and south winds which prevail ensure the island a plentiful rainfall (averaging 984.5 milimetres a year) and, because of this, it has lush vegetation and many springs. Snow is a rare phenomenon on the island.

A typically Zakynthian well.

The imposing west coast.

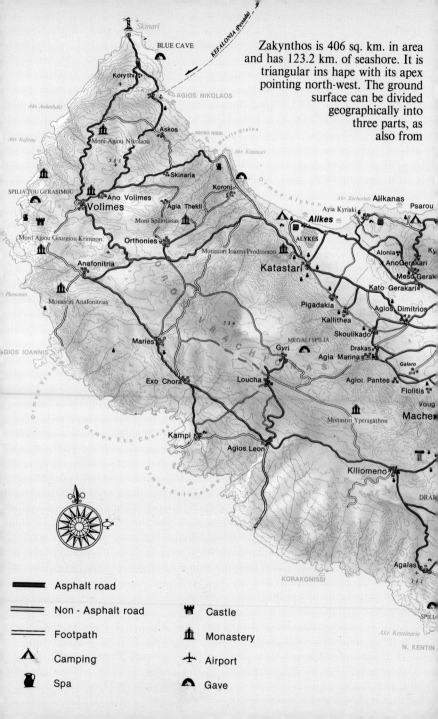

Zakynthos is 406 sq. km. in area and has 123.2 km. of seashore. It is triangular ins hape with its apex pointing north-west. The ground surface can be divided geographically into three parts, as also from

▬▬	Asphalt road
═══	Non - Asphalt road
───	Footpath
▲	Camping
♟	Spa
♜	Castle
🏛	Monastery
✈	Airport
⌂	Gave

a Geological stand point, going from north to south.

The first part begins at the northern Cape Skinari and progresses south, encompassing all the western part of the island, to the southwestern Cape Marathia. This area is sparsely populated and dominated by Mt Vrachionas (756 metres high).

The middle part starts from the north, from the Bay of Alikes and ends at the Bay of Lagana, taking in the fertile plain of the town of Zakynthos. It is flat, with very fertile land, and here we find the majority of the islands 400,000 inhabitants.

The third part takes up the eastern and southeastern side of the island, up to the southern Cape Yeraki, where we find Mt. Skopos (492 metres) and its foothills. There are no rivers on the island, only water courses that run with streams in the rainy season.

HISTORY

Prehistory

Although the ancient writers attest that Zakynthos was inhabited during the fifteenth and sixteenth centuries BC —Thucydides mentions that the first settlers were Achaians from the Peloponnese—.

Other versions of prehistoric times have been formulated, which bring us up to the 10th century BC and are based on the findings of Gerakas, Vasilikos, Alikes, etc.

One of these traditional accounts, mentioned also by Homer, tells of Zakynthos, son of Dardanos, the ancestor of the kings of Troy (whose parents were Zeus and Atlas' daughter Elektra) arriving with men and ships from the Arcadian town of Psophida, building and fortifying and acropolis which he called Psophida.

Pliny quotes another tradition, according to which the island was originally called Iria, after earlier settlers led by the Arcadian hero Irieas.

The general conclusion seems to be that the first inhabitants of Zakynthos came from the Peloponnese, even though one school of thought believes Pliny's Iria to be the Iria in Boeotia.

There have been various theories concerning the origin of the name Zakynthos, besides that given by Homer. The scholar Wood derives it from the words *za*, which is ancient Greek for town, and *kynhtos*, meaning hill, and justifies his opinion by the hilly topography of the island. Another scholar believes —albeit mistakenly— that the name originated with the hyacinth flower which has been known to grow on the island for as long as there are records. Other researchers have found variants of the name Zakynthos, such as Diakynthos, Iakynthos, Diakythos, Zakyta and, written in Latin characters, Jacinthum, Jantes, Lesante, Giante, Creti, Ganti, Sante and others, which latter names appear to be corruptions or misrenderings.

A mythological tale tries to account for the cults of Apollo and Artemis on Zakynthos. It tells of how Artemis, goddess of wild life and virgin huntress, loved roaming the rich forests of Zakynthos, while her brother Apollo, god of light and music but also of archery, was equally charmed by the island and sat among the laurel trees with his followers, playing the lyre. The worship of these two gods on Zakynthos, as also of Dionysus and Aphrodite, took the form of grand festivals and contests in their honour.

When the Arcadian settlers arrived on the island, they built fortifications and prospered sufficiently to be able to send out colonists of their own. Their ships took them to the shores of Spain, where they founded a daughter city which they called Zakantha. This became a flourishing commercial and cultural town which prospered for more than a thousand years. In 218 BC it was besieged by Hannibal and a force of 15,000 soldiers. The inhabitants bravely withstood the siege for eight months and managed to inflict considerable damage on Hannibal's forces. In the end, hunger forced them to make a desperate break-out. Hannibal proceeded to level the whole of Zakantha to the ground, leaving only the temple of Artemis, who was worshipped in the colony as she had been in the mother-city.

A vase painting showing Odysseus slaying the suitors of Penelope (5th century BC).

Other settlers from Zakynthos founded the town of Kidonies on Crete, a colony on Paros island and, jointly with the Phocaeans, the town of Phokida (or Parnassia) on the Pyrrenean headland in Spain.

Later on in the prehistoric period, Zakynthos was successively ruled by Arkeisios, king of Kephalonia, by Laertis and Laertis' son Odysseus, Homer's king of Ithaca.

Odysseus' people —from Ithaki, Kephalonia, Lefkada and Akarnania— sent a total of twelve ships to the war with Troy, and Homer in the Iliad is not sparing with his praises of their courage. He refers to them under the general name of "Kephalines". After the end of the Trojan War and when Odysseus had finally returned to Ithaca, Homer tells of the destruction by Odysseus of his wife Penelope's importunate suitors. The account in the Odyssey mentions the killing of twenty young men from Zakynthos.

It seems that Homer's tale of the suitors reflects what was in fact a revolt of the islands, which resulted in the end of Odysseus' rule over them. Neoptolemus (who at Troy had killed king Priam) was the intermediary who organised the signing of a treaty giving the islands their independence in return for an annual tribute tax. The Neoptolemus treaty was the first such in Greek history which established the independence of a country and provided for its democratic rule.

The historical period

No information on Zakynthos has come to us on the beginnings of the historical period.

Zakynthos played no significant role in antiquity, despite the fact that it was a rich and commerccially prosperous island. It owed its commercial development to its geographical location and to its bitumen springs. Silver coins minted in the 6th century AD, depicting the sacred symbol of the trident, indicate that the islanders worshiped the cult of Apollo.

A Zakynthian stater (5th century BC).

Beyond certainty the island did not take part in the Persian Wars of the 6th century BC. This is inferred from Herodotus' account of two Lacedaemonian traitors, Dimaratos and Igisistratos, trying to take refuge on Zakynthos. The first of them was expelled from the island by the Zakynthians, and the second was handed over to his fellow countrymen.

During the years of the struggle for supremacy between the two great powers of Greece, Athens and Sparta, which preceded the Peloponnesian War between them and their allies, the inhabitants of Zakynthos at first allied with the Lacedaemonians. But around 456 BC the Athenian fleet, under its commander Tolmidis, laid waste the Laconian shores and forced the Zakynthians, as well as other allies of Sparta, to join with Athens. When armed hostilities broke out between Kerkyra (Corfu) and Corinth —which were one of the immediate causes for the subsequent war— Zakynthos sent a thousand soldiers to the assistance of Kerkyra. They distiguished themselves by their valour and helped win the sea battle of 434 BC, wihch took place off Lefkimi on the coast of Corfu.

When the Lacedaemonians had recovered from the early defe.ts inflicted on their naval forces by Athens and had begun to build up a proper fleet, they sent the Spartan general Knymos with a hundred ships to conquer Zakynthos in 430 BC. His sizeable fleet notwithstanding, Knymo was obliged to withdraw in the face of strong resistance.

Next the Zakynthians are known to have sent ships with the Sicilian campaign in 415 BC (the last pajor phase of the Peloponnesian War), which ended with the crushing defeat of the Athenians in 413. The Athenian alliance fell apart shortly afterwards, and Zakynthos once more found itself under Lacedaemonian domination. It even exchanged its democratic constitution for an oligarchic one. However, by the time of the treaty between the Athenians and the Lacedaemonians of 371 BC, which stipulated as a basic condition the autonumy of all Greek cities, Zakynthos had discovered its freedom and its democratic rule.

The Roman Periode

A Roman coin of Zakynthos (2nd c. BC).

During the Macedonian wars (215-205 and 200-197 BC), Zakynthos tried again to remain neutral, just as it had done in the Persian Wars. It did not succed.

The island fell first to the Macedonians, then to the Romans, and then again to the Macedonians, who eventually gave Zakynthos to King Aminandras of the Athamanoi.

By decree of Aminandros, the tyrants Phillipos of Megalopoli and Ieroklis of Akraganda, were made rulers of the island.

Archaeological research and the testimony of ancient writers prove that on Zakynthos, an impressive civilization flourished from ancient times.

Of these, there is a marble ensemble depicting Apollo, Aphrodite and Artemis, found near the Zakynthos castle (where the ancient acropolis was situated) which today stands in the Tiepolo museum in Venice.

Other finds include some ancient coins and the ruins of ancient buildings (the temple of Apollo and Artemis, the tomb of Kikerona, etc.).

From the moment the first Roman occupation of the island ended, Rome tried hard to get Zakynthos back, appreciating not only its geographical advantages for commerce and conquests, but also its inhrerent wealth and the capabilities of its people.

Meanwhile, Zakynthos had been ruled by three tyrants in succession, and in 191 BC the aristocratic Ieroklis sold the island to the Achaians. However, Titus Flaminius who was to become Roman consul a few years later, happened to be present at the assembly of the Achaians at which Zakynthos was to change hands. Arguing that the island had actually been given to Rome as a war prize, and making the most of his oratorial talents, Flaminius managed to win Zakynthos back for Rome.

This did not, however, please the people of Zakynthos, and they organised an insurrection. The outraged Romans promptly dispatched a naval force to teach the islanders a lesson. They burned and destroyed whatever they could, and posted a garrison on Zakynthos. Not long after the main party had left, however the Zakynthians, with the help of the Aetolians, drove the Roman garrison off the island again. The Roman reaction was swift. They sent off their general Fulvius, who vanquished the Aetolians and reconquered Zakynthos in 150 BC. He imposed local self-government on the Zakynthians, and forbade them any alliances with out-siders.

Fulvius' strategy seems to have borne fruit, and the Roman overlords and the local population learnt to live with each other in mutual give and take. This was demonstrated when Mithridates VI, Eupator, King of Pontus and an indefatigable enemy of Rome, sent his general Archelaos to take Zakynthos. On this occasion the islanders fought stoutly at the side of the Roman soldiers, and Archelaos had finally to call off the siege of Zakynthos and sail off home in 87 BC without having achieved his purpose.

The pirate activities of the pre-Christian years brought successive invasions of the island, mainly by Sicilian corsairs. In 67 BC Rome charged Pompey (who was to become Pompey the Great) with ridding the Mediterranean of the pirate scourge, a task he accomplished successfully (before going on to utterly defeat Mithridates). In 36 BC, Zakynthos was given to Mark Antony, but after his defeat at the battle of Actium the island came into the possession of Octavian, heir of Caesar and the sole survivor of the Second Triumvirate.

At the redistribution of the Roman provinces, Zakynthos was made part of the province of Achaia, which included Epirus, the Peloponnese, and all the Greek islands except Crete. To begin, with, the government was by pro-consuls. When later the Romans insisted that the island govern itself again independently under its own laws, Zakynthos had to pay an annual tax to Rome and provide a certain number of men for Roman legions. In those years the island developed apace both materially and culturally, and achieved such a standing that it could regularly invite famous scholars from Rome to lecture and teach.

There is no conclusive evidence to fix the time in which Christianity spread to Zakynthos. It is, however, infered that the conversion to the faith could not have taken place before the middle of the 3rd century AD.

The Byzantine period

The decline and fall of the Roman empire gave a fresh impetus to the pirates and to other would-be conquerors, who all renewed their attacks on Zakynthos. For decades, Barbary corsairs, Goths, Vandals, Huns and other hordes scourged Zakynthos and the other Eptanissos islands of the Ionian and the western Mediterranean generally. They plundered, murdered and destroyed ruthlessly, the stubborn resistance of the local inhabitants notwithstanding. Wave after wave of raiders overran the islands, stripped them bare, and left only to return in due course in ever greater strength.

When Constantine the Great (c. 274-337 AD) founded the Byzantine empire, Zakynthos became part of the province of Illyria, governed by a reserve officer who had been assigned full powers.

Although under the protection of Constantinople —Constantine's name for his new seat of government, formerly known as the city of Byzantium— the island had somewhat less to suffer from the destructive raids of the pirates. After Constantine's death his squabbling successors neglected the outlying parts of the empire, and the raids and the plundering resumed in full force.

In terms of social organisation in the Byzantine era, the people of Zakynthos belonged to one of three classes. In the top class were the epiphaneis (upper crust), the big landowners of the island, the second class was comprised of artisans and merchants, and the third class consisted of farmers, who were further subdivided into those who owned their land, into leaseholders, and serfs.

Christianity came to Zakynthos early. There is a local tradition that in

A painting from the dependency of St Catherine of Mt Sinai (by Damaskinos, 16th c.).

34 AD Mary Magdalene came to the island en route from Jerusalem to Rome, and her ship anchored for a while on the westen coast of Zakynthos where she preached the teachings of Jesus of Nazareth.

There is still a village in that part of the island called Maries, where the memory is celebrated every year with a special festival.

Zakynthos suffered extensive destruction in 466, when the African Vandal king Gizarich arrived with sixty ships and his men fell to plunder, rape and slaughter, and set fire to Zakynthos town.

When Gizerich left, he took with him five hundred of the "upper crust" landowners, whom he butchered as his ships sailed out into the Adriatic and flung their bodies overboard.

One characteristic of Byzantine Zakynthos, however, is the continuity of Westen influnce in its administration, in contrast to the rest of Greece. It must be remembered that the island belonged to Rome until the 8th century AD.

The years that followed brought new pirate raids, by the Saracens this time, and new catastrophes.

In 844 Byzantium sent out its commander Nikitas, and later on his deputy Nassar, who between them freed the island from the raiders who received harsh punishment.

Around this time Zakynthos and Cephalonia were taken out of the province of Achaia and placed in the 11th district of Longovarda. Later still, a specifically Byzantine district of Cephalonia was formed, which included all the seven Ionian isles.

The Crusaders and Frankish rule (1185-1485)

By the time the Byzantine empire was drawing to its close, the appetite of the European aristocracy for conquests in easten lands had been growing rapidly, fed by increasingly ambitious ruthlessness. Under the pretext of liberating the Holy Land from the heathens, crusader aimies of adventurers and booty-hunters swarmed to invade the riches of the East.

On the way home from one such crusade, the Norman noble Voimonde fell with insane fury on the Eptanissos islands, intent on revenging the failure of his father Giscard to take Zakynthos and Cephalonia in 1084. Once more Zakynthos was laid in ruins.

In 1147 the Normans came again, led by Rogiro 1, and occupied all the Ionian isles. Although Emperor Emanuel of Byzantium managed with the help of the Venetians to take the islands back, he was eventually forced to sign a peace treaty with Rogiro in 1158.

In 1185 Zakynthos and Cephallonia broke away finally from the Byzantine empire. They formed the palatinate of Cphalonia and Zakynthos, which was maintained for three whole centuries, until 1479, initially under the rule, or overlordship of the Orsini family, then of the Angenins, and subsequently by Leonardo De Tocci and his descendents.

The innumerable escapades of the Orsinis, the generally unsettled times in which they ruled and their determined efforts to retain the palatinate at all costs, meant that they badly neglected the organization and administration of their domain, concerning themselves exclusively with ensuring their sovereignty. The need to remain in favour with Rome and its papal rulers, who could guarantee their protection, pushed the Orsinis into forcing Catholicism on the islanders and doing away with the Bishoprics on Zakynthos and Cephallonia. Inevitably, as in all Frankish controlled Greece, there followed the persecution of the Orthodox clergy and repression of the Orthodox population. The Catholic clergy were given a free hand and indulged themselves arbitrarily.

In 1209, Mathaio Orsini accepted Venetian overlordship for Zakynthos and Cephallonia. Subsequently these two islands became part of the Geoffrey de Villehardouin who ruled Achaia, and thereafter the counts of Zakynthos and Cephallonia were subordinate to the princes of Achaia.

Matthaio Orsini's second son, Richard, who married Anna Komninou, daughter of the Epirus despot Ioannis Angelos, was killed at Glarentza in 1303. He was succeded by his son, Giovanni 1, who married Maria, daughter of the despot Nikiphoros, and sister of the last Greek despot of Epirus, Thomas Komninos.

During Giovanni's rule, the Catalans established a settlement on Zakynthos. Thomas Komninos was succeded by Nikolaos, who left the administration of the earldom of Zakynthos-Cephallonia in the hands of his brother, Giovanni II. Nikolaos killed Thomas' uncle and made himself despot of Epirus, abandoning the Western Christian dogma for Eastern orthodoxy. He was murdered in turn by his brother Giovanni II who, on acquiring Epirus, also adopted the orthodox faith, married Anna Palaiologou, and Hellenised his name to Ioannis-Angelos Komninos. When his ambitious wife poisoned him in 1355, the Orsini line came to an end.

Before his death Ioannis-Angelos Komninos had been forced to recognise Philip I, King of Naples, as suzerain of Zakynthos and the other islands. At his death, Philip bequeathed these lands to his eldest son and heir, Roberto.

When Roberto was imprisoned after losing a war, the brothers Leonardo, Petro and Ludovico de Tocci helped him to escape. To show his gratitude, Roberto gave Leonardo the princupality of Zakynthos and Cephallonia, Ithaki and Echinades, as well as his sister Francesca as wife. In this way the de Tocci dynasty was founded, which was to govern the island for more than a century.

The new rulers, equally ambitious but more capable than their predecessors succeeded in increasing the possessions of the palatinate, seizing lands in Epirus (on the Greek mainland). At the same time, they managed to organize the administration and finances of the island, bestowing on the region a period of peace and stability. The population of Zakynthos grew to 25,000 inhabitants, nearly equalling the 30,000 of today.

Leonardo I did what he could to further the overall development of the Ionian islands, and set them firmly on the road to progress and prosperity. Most of his work was undone again by his successor, Carlos I, who was a selfish leader, unloved by the people, insatiable, violent and ever looking for war. His military exploits plus his marriage to the daughter of the Duke of Athens extended his possessions to include Arta, Akarnania, Albania, Achaia and Glarentza. Carlos' Greek subjects breathed a little more freely towards the end of his life, when he entrusted the government of the islands to his brother Leonardo II.

Carlos I died in Ioannina in 1429, and appointed as his successor his nephew Carlos ll, who rejoiced in the title "By the Grace of God, Lord of Arta, Duke of Lefkada, Count of the Palatinate of Cephallonia, Ithaki and Zakynthos".

His successor, Leonardo III, an unstable opportunist, kept fighting the Turks —sometimes winning, sometimes losing— and eventually signed a peace treaty with them under which Zakynthos was obliged to pay an annual tax to the Porte. When the tax was left unpaid, the Turks sent their fleet to sack the island. "Faced with the oncoming Ottoman fleet", says Georgios Frantzis in his "Chronicles", "*Leonardo abandoned Zakynthos and left under cover of night*". He took his treasury with him.

The intervention of the Venetians ensured a delay in the Turkish landing, chiefly so as to give the Frankish inhabitants of the island the chance to leave. The pillage finally took place in September 1479, and henceforth a Turkish garrison was quartered on Zakynthos.

The Venetians, who at this time were busily expanding their possessions and influence in the Mediterranean, had for some time been aware of the value and significance of Zakynthos. In 1485 they persuaded the Porte to cede them the island, in return for an annual five-hundred gold ducats to be paid to the Sultan.

A engraved map of Zakynthos (17th century, from the collection of D. Zivas).

Venetian Rule (1484-1797)

The agreement of 1484 brought fundamental changes to Zakynthos and ushered in a new epoch for its people. Until then, the island's fate had been part of that of the rest of Greece, and Zakynthos had physically and psychologically belonged to the body of Greece as a whole—even if that body was repeatedly dismembered, or the ties between the inhabitants of Zakynthos and other Greeks were not always those of friendship and patriotic support. After the disaster of September 1479, Zakynthos stood alone and in ruins.

Shortly after the Venetian takeover, the handful of islanders who had survived the holocaust saw the arrival of thousands of new settlers. Venice had issued announcements in 1485 and 1492 in all its territories, inviting whoever wished to come to Zakynthos and make a new home. The Venetian nobles who held the reigns of government in Zakynthos generously shared out the farms and houses amongst the newcomers. A new period of activity began, which quickly resulted in high population growth: the records of 1515 could testify to more than 20,000 people living in Zakynthos.

An important feature of this demographic development was that the Zakynthian element was by no means wiped out. On the contary, it not only recovered to a remarkable degree, but its influence was such that it assimilated the newcomers and permeated them with the characte- ristics of its own local traditions. Part of the reason for the growing prosperity of the island was, of course, that Venetian rule created conditions of peaceful stability such as had not been known for centuries.

One result of this was that the typical medieval settlement of Zakynthos which had been huddling close to the defensive strength of the castle, began to expand outside the walls and in time became a major town on the seaward slopes, with well planned streets, open squares, and impossing buildings. Known under the name of Aegialos, this fine new town came to be dubbed by the people of the time the "Florence of Greece".

Emboldened by Venetian protection, the islanders also began to establish, at first semipermanent and later permanent, settlements elsewhere on the island.

The growth of the town, the promulgation of new laws, and the resurgence of commercial activities laid the foundation for the proper social organisation of the island along communal lines, in a manner unknown since the fall of the ancient world.

The usual aristocratic-oligarchic constitution of the Venetians provided for the self-government of Zakynthos under a Council of Nobles, who elected their Prince as well as a general Governor who dealt with day-to-day administrative, judicial and military matters.

As in all Venetian-ruled territories, the population was divided into three classes:

— The nobility (**nobili**), whose income derived from their landed estates, and whose fathers and grandfathers had at no time engaged in the "coarse pursuits", i.e. manual labour. The members of this class were registered in the Golden Book, the Libro d'Oro.

— The citizens (**civili**), the middle class of prosperous merchants teachers, goldsmiths, priests, notaries, and other professional men, who had no political rights. Although it was their dream and ambition that their names should eventually be inscribed in the Libro d'Oro and their descendants become members of the nobility, they frequently stood up for the right of the common people.

— The common people (**popolari**), who were divided into workers, farm labourers, sailors and, more generally, all those engaged in "coarse pursuits". They had no political rights and, according to a very courageous admission by a Venetian (Ermo Lucci) their status was, in real fact, that of serfs. The farm labourers were the most exploited of all, since they had only obligations and no rights. Besides the financial support they gave the island (the economy was mainly agriculture-based) they could also be conscripted to defend the island against enemy invasion. The Venetian rulers exploited them shamelessly and mercilessly.

Despite this, they remained loyal to Venice because they realized that Greeks elsewhere suffered far more under Turkish rule.

It was indeed the insatiable and inhumane rapaciousness of the nobility which in time led to serious social opposition and friction. By the beginning of the seventeeth century, this unrest had become so acute that it led to the first social revolution in modern Greek history. The 1628-1632 Revolt of the People was drowned in its own blood by the Venetian Governor of the time.

Meanwhile the Zakynthians had frequently to fend off attacks from the Turks, sometimes fighting alone, sometimes alongside their neighbours. Zakynthos sent its own ships and troops to the sea battle of Nafpaktos in 1571, when the Christian fleet secured a major victory againnst the Porte.

After the Cretan War in 1669 and the occupation of Crete by the Turks, many Cretan families left their homeland. Among those who escaped to Zakynthos were the forebears of the national Greek poet Dionysios Solomos.

The Republic of Venice was declining markedly. The impotence and greed of many of its nobles, most of whom lived in the overseas territories, increasingly provoked the protest and revolution of the lower classes who suffered the brunt of ever greater injustice, deprivation and persecution.

Biding their time with ill-concealed impatience, the Turks were hovering expectantly, while new powers were coming into the ascendancy in Europe.

One by one Venice lost her overseas possessions. Her power was shrivelling, and everlasting feuds among her worthless nobles brought her to the edge of ruin. The people of Zakynthos watched this visible decline of its rulers and waited for the opportunity to cast off their yoke.

With the spead of 18th century French liberal ideas and in the wake of the French Revolution, the people of Europe threw off the lethargy of subordination and organised themselves in the pursuit of the ancient human rights of freedom, equality and national independence, which had been so barbarically trampled on for centuries on end.

Zakynthos received the new French ideas with enthusiasm. By the time Napoleon was winning his bat-tles, political groups were being form-ed on the island, the most important among them the 'Club of the Jacobins'. Its members included two literary men of note, the pre-Solomos poet Antonios Martelaos, and the dramatist Dimitrios Gouzelis. The fundamental goals of the Zakynthos Jacobins were their complete political equality with the nobility.

The ruling class on the island not unnaturally reacted negatively to this liberal movement. They were fully aware of the dangers these new ideas presented for their own class, and they had no compunction in stamp-ing out very few voices of dissent when it was decided to murder all the Jacobins.

A water-colour of Zakynthos by Buondelmonti (16th c., Gennadios Library, Athens).

Adminstrative seals of Zakynthos on official

The years of the French Republic (1797)

Despite the bloodthirsty stand of the ruling nobility on Zakynthos, the glorious Republic of San Marco had run its course. The last Venetian Governor surrendered the town and the island to the French on 14 July 1797. The local people celebrated the end of the oppression by pouring into the streets and squares, joyously singing and dancing. Their euphoric celebration reached its climax on 30 July 1797, when they publicly burnt the Golden Book in the triangular square of St Mark, together with the coats-of-arms of the nobility, hated symbols of local oppression, and planted a 'Tree of Freedom'.

The French Consul, Charles de Guy, temporarily undertook the administration of Zakynthos, and formed a municipal council which was barred to members of the nobility. This council immediately voted the abolition of all aristocratic titles, and divided the island into communities administered by local mayors.

Stripped of all direct power, the demoted nobles had only subversion to fall back on. They tried to foster anarchy by spreading the rumour that republican-minded Zakynthians were organising a reactionary stand again-st the French. When the nobles were threatened with expulsion from the island, they made a gift of a large sum of money to the French military, and so managed to delay the decision for their ouster.

Under the French, Zakynthos became the administrative headquarters of the Prefecture of the Aegean, and the democratic government began the difficult task of reconstruction. An important feature of this period was the establishment of schools for children from all the social classes. The first French presence on the island lasted only 15 months.

Russo-Turkish domination

Even though all over Europe the winds of democracy were blowing away the old order the monarchical powers were doing all they could to reverse the trend. Turkey, England, Russia, Portugal and Naples managed to drive the French out of the eastern territories; the Russians and the Turks prepared to take Zakynthos. At this point the fallen nobles, who a few months previously had branded the people of Zakynthos as reactionaries against the French, did not hesitate to turn round and denounce

documents issued by the various occupying authorities (1787-1852).

them for heartily supporting the French. By clever subversion and liberal outlays of money, they even succeeded in rousing several villages to move against the French garrison on the island.

On 25 October 1798, after a siege by the Russo-Turkish fleet, and after some of the pro-Russian nobles had handed the keys of the town to the besiegers, the French garrison was forced to surrender. This was followed by much violence between the nobles and the people, deliberately incited by provocators.

Meanwhile the aristocracy managed to recover many of its privileges. Fearing, however, that the support of their new lords minght not be sufficient to ensure the long and secure return to power, they began to look for support from the English.

The Ionian State

On 21 March 1800, Russia and Turkey signed a treaty in Constantinople which founded the Eptánissos State of the Ionian Isles. This State, according to the terms of the treaty, was to be a self-governing part of the Russian empire, and would pay an annual tax to the Porte in Constantinople.

This treaty provided the nobles of Zakynthos with a new opportunity for furthering their schemes for power. They sent a delegation to Constantinople as ambassadors of the Eptánissos State, who saw to it that a 'constitution' was devised to lay down the principle for the government of the islands. This constitution stipulated that the Ionian islands should be a confederation, and that each island was to be administered by a local government, the members of which were to be drawn exclusively from the 'hereditary nobility'.

The people of Zakynthos did not agree, and they began to revolt. One of their democratic leaders, Antónios Martinégos, organised a movement which declared the island independent of the Eptanissos confederation. Playing on the acquisitive tendency of the English, they hoisted the Union Jack on the Zakynthos fortress on 10 February 1801. But the hopes of the Zakynthos democrats had been premature. Seven months and a number of strange agreements between the Great Powers later, the Turks and, to the chagrin of the Zakynthians, the English, returned the island to the Ionian State.

The nobles for their part continued their machinations, which resulted in several new constitutions, each more contradictory than the last, and eventually in another two years of rule by France, this time under the Emperor Napoleon.

Ayiou Markou Square (the 'Platyforos'), a lithograph from

*artwright, 'Views in the Ionian Islands' *(1821).*

The English Rule (1809-1864)

Eight years after the Zakynthos' democrats' unsuccessful bid to bring in the English, three English frigates with 3,000 soldiers sailed into Zakynthos on 19 September 1809, took the fortress and hoisted the English flag.

To begin with the English carried out a series of beneficial measures for the daily life and administration of the island, especially with regard to public health, which until then had been badly neglected, particularly among the lower classes. Another important event of that time was the foundation of a public printing-house in Zakynthos which, among other publications, brought out the "Newspaper of the Free Islands".

A characteristic description was recorded by the French traveller Buchon: *"The roads of Zakynthos are very well-paved and well-lit. The local government has taken great pains to see to the building of roads, the lighting, the availability of water fountains and the cleanliness of the town".*

J. Cartwright, the seafront at Zakyntho(s)

In 1814 England, Russia, Austria and Prussia agreed that the islands of the Ionian should become independent and form the United State of the Ionian Isles. The English made sure of retaining for themselves exclusively the "protection" of the islands — which meant, essentially, the government. An English High Commissioner was appointed, with his seat in Corfu. A new constitution of 1817 laid the groundwork for tyrannical behaviour by the English, and the people began to rebel again. The first High Commissioner, Thomas Maitland, proved inflexible, violent and unjust, and the Eptánissos islands were once more the victims of their overlords' selfseeking.

The people of Zakynthos now began a number of moves against the British empire. On 23 February 1821 they despatched a petition to George IV, King of England, asking for the revision of the oppressive constitution. The petition was signed by thirty-two leading personalities of Zakynthos, including the chief prosecutor and legislator of the Ionian State, Anastássios Flambouriáris.

the estuary of the Ayios Haralambos river (I. Cartwright, 1863).

Although this particular petition had little effect, it was important for being the first of a series of official complaints and accusations by the people of Zakynthos against the English oppressors.

When the **Philiki Etairia**, or the 'Society of Friends' was formed to help free Greece from foreign rule, the people of Zakynthos were eager to cooperate and to give any help they could. 'Etairia' representatives Pangalos, and later Aristidis Papas, came to the island and enrolled active members, founding the so-called Zakynthos Fighting Committee. The far-reaching activities of this committee earned it the name of the 'Ministry of the Exterior of Revolutionary Greece'. President of the committee was Dionyssios Romas, and its members included Konstantinos Dragonas, Panayiotis Stephanou, Anastassios Flambouriaris, N. Kolivas and Frangiskos Karvelas. They took their oath of allegiance in the little church of Aghios Georgios on the Psiloma hill above the town on the way to the castle, in the presence of the Epirote priest Anthimos Argiropoulos.

The town of Zakynthos in a lithograph of [

7. D'Osteruald, La Grèce. 'Vues P., Pittoresques et topographiques').

Men from Zakynthos took part in the battles of Tripoli, Neokastro, Lala, Peta and others, and especially at Missolonghi, where Zakynthos ships frequently broke through the blockade and took food and ammunition to the besieged.

The English occupation marked the zenith of prosperity for the island. Bridges built at this time are still standing today and continue to serve the island's transportation network. Part of the port's sea wall dates back to this period. The English also built many mansions on the outskirts of town on the old Venetian estates and undertook the restoration of, and additions to village churches, with their ever-present and imposing bell towers. Of the many other houses built by the English on Zakynthos, not a trace remains today.

The church of Aghios Georgios of the Philikon saw the swearing-in not only of local Zakynthians, but also of freedom fighters from elsewhere. Among them were such renowned men as Kolokotronis, Nikitaras, Plapoutas, Grivas, Zacharias, Photomaras, Martelaos, Dimadis, Gouzelis, Dalostros, the Petimezades and others.

When the Greek revolution was openly declared, the people of Zakynthos swelled with fresh hopes of liberation. Thousands of them went to the Peloponnese to fight by the side of their fellow Greeks, even though the English had strictly forbidden any assistance whatsoever to the insurgents. The 'Zakynthos Fighting Committee' achieved miracles. It provided asylum on the island for many refugees and sent money and men to support the cause.

St George 'Filikon'.

The end of foreign rule: Union with Greece (1864)

British rule still held firm on Zakynthos and the other Ionian islands, however, not only during the revolution, but even after the liberation and the establishment of the young Greek State. It was Britain's formal recognition of Free Greece —albeit within the limited boundaries imposed by the Great Powers— which heralded the start of new persistent struggles by the island peoples.

Their first step was to succeed in securing certain reforms of the constitution. The removal of censorship and the grant of a number of civil rights permitted the formation of three political parties on Zakynthos: the Radicals, the Reformers, and the Plutocrats. The Radicals represented the broad and progressive layers of the people, and had as their main objective the banishment of the English 'protectors' and the union of the Ionian islands with Greece. The Reformers were more moderate, and merely advocated improved government under the English. The Plutocrats were the tools of the English. They formed the English-Ionian Association, and were known by their opponents as 'The Fiends', or 'The Retrogrades'.

The proportion of representatives voted into the Ionian Parliament by the first free elections of 28 February 1850 was a direct reflection of popular sentiment: 30 Radicals, 6 Plutocrats, and 4 Reformers.

Although the English and their associates began a reign of persecution, dismissals, banishments and other measures of blackmail, Member of Parliament Ioannis Tipaldos-Kapeletos proposed on 2 December 1851 that the Ionian Parliament should vote on the union of the Eptanissos islands with Greece. Tough reprisals from the English followed this proposal, but the ethnic passions and determination of the people could no longer be held in check. Their struggles were now coordinated by the dynamic and fearless Member of Parliament and leader of the Radicals, Konstantinos Lombardos.

Notwithstanding all the delays and obstacles the reactionary powers could contrive, the struggle of the Eptanissos isles for freedom were finally vindicated. On 5 June 1863 a treaty was signed in London by England, France and Russia, under which England had to abandon her status as protector power and on **21 May 1864**, the Greek flag was raised on the the castle of Zakynthos and the people jubilantly celebrated their union with Greece.

Now a part of Free Greece, Zakynthos and the other Ionian islands shared the ensving course of history with the rest of the country.

In the twentieth century, the new social, political and economic conditions that prevailed contributed to the definitive deterioration of the island. That which remained after 1900 was only the facade of the island's past grandeur. A facade which only hinted at the quality and quantity of this grandeur but still expressed a strong popular tradition whose presence often surprises us today. The earthquake of 1953 was a fateful event which destroyed even the facade. A visitor today who wishes to discover traces of the past and to acquaint himself with Zakynthos' artistic heritage must not confine himself to the main town but travel widely throughout the island.

TODAY AND YESTERDAY

In the preceding chapters we referred to the physical characteristics of the island. To really get to know Zakynthos however, we must get into her rhyhm; take a look at the people, at how they lived in the past and how they live now.

During the period in which the Venetians ruled the area, Zakynthos was at peace and, as a center of trade, enjoyed a prosperous development. Under these favourable conditions, a confident middle class slowly emerged and proceeded to demand more rights.

The ruling nobility defended itself against this encroachment however, and there ensued a period of intense social confrontation which led to the "People's Revolt" of 1628 (see page 20) Economic development, social struggle and the simultaneous arrival of Cretans bringing with them much initiative and creative talent resulted in an intellectual blossoming on the island, consolidated during the years of the French Revolution, at the end of the 18th century.

This political evolution, with its many fierce struggles, played an important role in shaping the character of the islanders.

In 1798, the French traveller Rulhiere described the common characteristics of the people of Zakynthos outlining their virtues and their weaknesses:

"Observing the moral makeup of a Zakynthian, one obvious characteristic dominates: it consists of a mix of natural virtues on the one hand and on the other, vices acquired under the rule of corrupt administrations. Watch him at a festival; he is joyful, ingenuous, full of life. His entire being expresses satisfaction, emerging, from the depths of his soul. He sings, dances and never loses his equilibrium. Enter his home; as long as he understands you have come without opportunistic intentions and arrogance, he welcomes you with affection and courtesy".

Through the centuries, these influences and social upheavals shaped the character of the Zakynthian one meets today in the towns and villages, trading in the markets, celebrating at the festivals, philosophizing at the Cafeneon; a cultured person, a lover of beauty, an individualist with his own peculiarities but also with his own sense of well-being, contented with life in his homeland — and in this he is justified. He is strangely nostalgic when away from his island and wherever he goes, he looks for something that reminds him of Zakynthos. It follows then, that this kind of individual would exhibit a certain equilibrium. After tending to the simple and monotonous duties of life, he wholeheartedly throws himself into his enjoyments. Pain and pleasure he transforms into verse; a song he sings either with laughter or with sorrow. He remains deeply attached to tradition and custom, or 'adetia' as he calls it in Greek (from the Turkish word, meaning tradition).

Each century has faithfully and inviolately copied from the one before it the 'adetia' (or, traditions) and every Zakynthian individually upholds these with reverence in his own personal way and never wavers in his allegiance. This personal way of upholding traditions is kept up with religious devotion and is repeated from year to year.

A rare engraving of Zakynthos before the earthquake, fro.

Customs and tradition on the island, however, suffered a severe disruption after the tragic earthquake of 1953. We have to go back 40 years, to Zakynthos as it was before the earthquake, in order to understand how that tragic event abrutly severed the island's historic continuity, obliterating not only the town itself but also much of the evidence that would have been useful today in ascertaining to what extent the old traditions had survived.

Before the war, Zakynthos was serviced by a mailboat that docked at the island there times a week, winter and summer. It left Piraeus at night, sailed through the Corinth canal, made a stop at dawn at Patras and round about midday reached Zakynthos town. One or two hours later it weighed anchor and headed on to Lixouri and Argostoli on the island of Cephalonia, where it tied up overnight. From there it began the return voyage over the Ionian sea, often accompanied by schools of dolphins.

Before entering the port of Zakynthos on its arrival, the mailboat would blow its horn 3 times. The long drawn out whistle brought all the towns people to the Strada Marina on the waterfront — those who were waiting for relatives to disembark as well as those without much to do who wanted just to find out who was coming and who was leaving the island. Then the usually empty Strada Marina came to life and buzzed with activity. The arrival of the boat was always an event on the island, as well as an opportunity for the local

ench magazine (late 19th century, from the collection of L. Merkati).

vendors, who invaded the boat with their decorated baskets offering for sale to the Cephalonians on board their special make of nougat, their powders, perfumes, icons and pamphlets on the life and miracles of Saint Dionysios, the patron saint of the island.

A gentle but persistent rivalry has always existed between the peoples of the two neighboring islands. The teasing and verbal playfullness between the Zakynthian 'Nionos' (the nickname for Diyonisos) and his counterpart from Cephalonia, 'Gerassimos', (the most common names on the two islands,) has given rise to many tales and anecdotes which illustrate the sparkling spirit of the islanders.

One of the most familiar of these tales, which contains some elements gleaned from real events, revolves around a fake canary belonging to a merchant from Zakynthos, and a Cephalonian with a counterfeit coin. It goes like this:

"A Zakynthian hawker boards the boat docked in the port with his wares, among which is a cage with a sparrow painted yellow. He shouts "canary for sale" and a Cephalonian returning to his island begins to bargain with him for it. The victim finally buys the bird for 5 drachmas. As the boat weighs anchor and slowly leaves the quay, Nionios shouts from the dock Gerassimos:
—If the bird sings, write to me...
The other shouts back from the boat:
— Nionios, if you can exchange that coin, write toy me..."

During the pre-war period, life on the island was more tranquil and peaceful, of course with many fewer comforts than today, but with its own special rhythm, now impossible to recover with the tempo of modern life. Descriptive recollections help us to imagine a Zakynthian home of distinction during this period.

"Night has fallen on Zakynthos. There is a mansion of the nobility lit up on Rougas Square, its green blinds partly drawn down over the windows, its enormous entrance-way flanked by classical Venetian stone columns, yellow with age.

"It is a holiday and the whole family is seated around the table in the beautifully decorated dining room. Hanging from the celing over the dining-room table is a splendid Venetian chandelier, its flickering light casting soft shadows over the room and the faces of the company. The candles dim glow, shining on the portaits of the family's ancestors hanging on the walls, makes them seem even more imposing with their wigs and high stiff collars, reminiscent of a time long past. A large 'rotonda', or round table also graces the dining room, with the addition of four cane rocking chairs.

"Beyond the dining room is the salon, with its old, heavy mahogany furniture and the large grand piano, with next to it the beautiful carved 'tazera', or ornamental shelf, decorated only with a silver candelabra and some other Venetian ornament of great value."

There were three types of houses in Zakynthos town: The large mansions (of the ruling nobility), the houses of the bourgoisie and those of the lower classes. The mansions were mainly built around the edge of town and in

The sitting-room of the Romas Mansion at 'Repara' destroyed in the '53 earthquake.

the suburb of 'repara', north of the municipal theatre (now the library) and on the seashore. The mansions usually had three floors with severe imposing facades of porous stone. On the first floor were the reception areas and on the second floor the bedrooms. There is insufficient evidence to allow a detailed description of the middle class and common houses. They probably had two or three floors with a wooden staircase leading up to the main living quarters. The exterior of these houses was influenced by that of the mansions, except for the first floor, which was built with a characteristic enclosed, wooden balcony called a 'bodzo', protruding over the street.

Today, all of this has changed. Post-earthquake Zakynthos has none of the beauty of the original town, despite the efforts made to rebuild it as faithfully as possible according to the original. There are no more old-style houses with their tiled roofs darkened with age. Instead, there are tall, freshly whitewashed buildings with modern balconies, large windows and spacious verandas which have little in common with the old, grand pre-1953 houses.

Only the town's newly-built museum still retains some elements of the old Zakynthos, contained in a number of exhibits which illustrate the grandeur of the religious, artistic and social culture of the Ionian islands. many of these exhibits were made possible only through the efforts of a man whom foreigners have dubbed "The Knight of the Ruins" -the pharmacist and scholar, and descendant of a noble family, Nikos Varvanis.

It is amazing what this exceptional Zakynthian achieved. While the earthquake was destroying the town and fire was engulfing everything, Varvianis, helped by a handful of Zakynthians, was scrambling through the ruins saving whatever he could of the remains of the old Zakynthos civilization. These he carefully collected and stored in an undisturbed corner of his estate, 'Hermitage', where they remained for a long time without anyone being aware of it. Thanks to Varvianis, one can still admire many of the traditional elements which help explain the history and special character of Zakynthos.

Tradition, however, is not only preserved in inanimate exhibits. It is also the expression of the soul; the social, religious and cultural manifestations in which the island is so rich. These particulars help us to understand the nature and idiosyncrasies of Zakynthos a little better.

One characteristic of the Zakynthian soul, and an inseperable companion of every islander, is *music* and *song*. The Zakynthians' love of music originated in ancient times and manifested itself at different historical periods. On the Zakynthos of classical-era Greece, the god of music, Apollo, was worshipped. One indication of how much the ancient Zakynthians revered music can be seen in the fact that the island minted a coin in honor of the musician Pythagoras, whose bust appeared on one side, with a lyre on the other.

Under the rule of the Venetians, the people became skillful players of a number of wind instruments, which they incorporated into their music for religious and military processions.

The islanders also developed a number of original musical forms all their own.

The Zakynthian *'cantada'*, a song for four voices in harmony, is still the most beloved of these. Another type of song, the *'arekia'*, reminds us of the Cretan influence on Zakynthian music. Despite what has been borrowed from Byzantine and Italian music, Zakynthos has clearly developed its own local Ionian island flavour, reflecting the island's cultural legacies.

A music school was founded there for the first time in 1815 by the Italian teacher **Marco Batayia**, and the following year the first Philharmonic orchestra was formed. Even these formal organizations were a natural outgrowth of tradition, since the people of Zakynthos had early on begun to gather together in choirs and other types of musical ensembles, developing their own talents and appreciation for music. Today the Zakynthos Philharmonic orchestra and the large musical associations, as well as the famous Zakynthian choir, carry on that tradition.

This musical growth over so many centuries has naturally produced gifted musicians recognized not only on Zakynthos and the Ionian islands, but even wider afield. An exceptional Zakynthian musician was **Franciscos Domeneginis** (1809-1874). Another famous guitarist and composer, **Andonis Kapnisis** (1813-1885) wrote marches, hymns, symphonies and choral pieces.

Pavlos Karrer (1829-1896), a composer of classical works, is known as the force behind modern Greek music. **Panayiotis Gritzanis**, earned fame as an inspired teacher and was the creative force behind the Ionian harmonies and sweet tones. Other composers of religious music on Zakynthos were **Pahomios Rousanos**, **Dionysios Lata** and last but not least on the list is **Ioannis Planiteros**.

The cantada was the most popular song in late 19th century Zakynthos.

Inextricably linked with music and song, and of perhaps even greater interest, are the popular dances of the island, the most famous of which is the Zakynthos 'sirtos'. A lively, spirited dance in two-quarters time, the 'sirtos' is performed in every village, where it is known by a variety of names — the *'levendiniko'*, *'galariotiko'*, *'volimiatiko'*, etc. It is danced to the accompaniment of tradition instruments — violin, accordion, and guitar, or 'tabourloniakaro' and the words of the songs speak mainly about love and marriage. In the mountain village of Aghios Leonda we find the 'amiri', a carnival dance, also performed in two-quarter time. The accompanying song recounts the misfortunes of a girl thrust into an unlucky marriage. The *'yiargitos' 'or dance of Theseus'*, is rarely performed, except in the village of Voughiato. The song, said to owe its origins to the ancient *'gerano'* described

The 'tambourloniariko' plays
a leading part in local festivities, enlivening the island's unique folk dances.

by Plutarch, is sung in three-quarter time, alternating with six-eighths, and describes the fight between Thesaeus and the Minotaur. The 'stavrotos' is performed at Katastari, Keri and in other mountain villages. It is danced to a two-fourths beat, with crossed hands in double lines. Finally, the 'kinigos', originating in Keri (a hunting village) is performed with the dancers holding shoulders, singing the song of the hunter and the nun. The movements to a number of other popular dances -'gaitani', 'rigotos', 'tsakistos', 'nifiatikos', 'panorios', etc. — were forgotten before they could be recorded, and have survived in name only.

Attending local festivals on Zakynthos was once a splendid, exuberant experience. The festivities today still retain some of this same livliness, particularly at Carnival time, before Lent. The Zakynthos 'carnival' was a product of Venetian society. The carnival period, which ends on the Sunday before the beginning of the lenten fast, was once a time of merrymaking and revelry for all the islanders and its customs developed in imitation of the splendid, popular festivals of Venice. During this period, dances were held at clubs, at people's homes, at local 'tavernas' and even outdoors, in squares and public places. **Square dances, quadrilles, polkas, mazourkas and waltzes were all performed with equal enthusiasm, as was the** 'yiargito', the 'gaiitani' (from a Turkish word meaning ribbon) and the 'tsakisto' (in which the dancers crouch suddenly, then leap to their feet).

The climax of the carnival began on Sunday afternoon, when the people gathered together in Zakynthos town's main St Marks square to enjoy the last night of revelry. There is the traditional "Funeral of the masks," a symbolic rite, and dancing continues until late in the evening in Solomos Square.

Drawings by K. Porfyris showing an 'omilia'.

40

An idea of how Zakynthians once dressed has been preserved in performances of the 'omilies' and in the costumes worn during carnival period and at local festivals. It is an impressive folkloristic element of Zakynthos and reflects the separation of the islanders over the decades into distinct social stratas.

The Zakynthian of yesterday dressed according to the neighbourhood in which they lived and thus according to their class. The nobility wore silk garments with jackets of thicker material, waistcoats, black hose, silk socks and soft shoes.

The ruling class wore wigs and shaved their beards and moustaches. Their women wore silk dresses with long trains. They also wore hats with masks or black veils, coloured stockings, shoes with buckles and gold bracelets.

The bourgeosie wore silk hats with tassels, hooded coats, coloured, knee-length trousers with 2 back pockets, silk socks and buckled shoes.

The common people wore trousers of a shiny Turkish fabric, waistcoats and sashes, white socks and buckled shoes. Their caps were white and they were forbidden to shave their beards or moustaches. The farmers were similary dressed, expect that they wore rough leather shoes called 'tsarouchia' and their coats were short and made of thick fabric. The sailors had their own specific dress; they wore coloured caps, crossover waistcoats with buttons and frills, red waistbands, wide trousers to the knees, white socks and buckled shoes.

The idiosycracies of a Zakynthian marriage are an interesting topic to explore. The customs, as they were followed in the past cannot be found elsewhere.

An old Zakynthian describes them as he himself has lived them:

"In order for a marriage to take place, the parents of the eligible youth discussed it together with the rest of the family and made all of the arrangements without either consulting or informing the young man of their decision. They chose a bride they considered suitable for their son and their family. The young boy, whether he agreed with the match or not, had to comply with his parent's decision without objection. In those days no matches were founded on love. This was not because of the lack of human feeling, but such was the custom, and

its observance required strict obediance. If, in those days, by some chance a young couple did have a love affair then the consequences were very ugly. The families would resort to murder — both the girl and boy were killed and often the whole family was broken up over the controversy. The marriage arrangements were initiated by a third person, the go-between, who was called the match maker.

Once the two sides had agreed on the dowry and all other matters with the match maker, a meeting was arranged for a Sunday, when every last detail concerning the dowry was written down on a sheet of paper called the Dowry Contract. This the future bridegroom kept. After this, arrangements were made for the father of the bridegroom to visit the house of the bride to meet his future daughter-in-law and her relatives.

Then, a few days later, the father of the bride would go to the house of the bridegroom to do the same thing. At this point, the arrangements for the actual wedding began. The father of the bride had to make ready the dowry he had promised. The bridegroom also had preparations to see to. When both families were ready, the date of the wedding was finalized.

In those days the wedding celebration usually began on a Monday and ended on a Sunday night a week later. Every night there was a feast with dancing and with different instrumental groups playing traditional music and songs.

As soon as the religious ceremony of marriage was over, everyone went to the house of the groom for the true wedding feast. Here the guests enjoyed themselves with much singing and dancing. Guns were traditionally fired into the air. At nightfall the relatives and guests began leaving, blessing the couple on their way out.

In those days the mother of the groom did not attend the wedding ceremony. She waited at home to welcome the newly weds and especially her new daughter-in-law. Horsemen traditionally raced from the church to announce to her the good news that the marriage was completed, and the first to arrive was given a gift of a special bread loaf, and a scarf was tied to his horse's ear. When the newly-weds arrived with all the relatives at the groom's house, then guns were fired into the air again. The groom's mother, waiting at the door of her home blessed the couple and especially the bride, to whom she fed a little sugar. This ritual feeding of sugar was supposed to ensure a 'sweet' relationship between them. As it is well known, very few new wives have loving realtions with their mothers-in-law!

The mother of the groom would have laid ready on the floor inside the door, a pair of man's trousers for the bride to step on. This was done in the hope of her having male children. A piece of iron was also conveniently placed for the bride to walk on, to ensure her bearing strong, healthy children, as well as a pomegranate to ensure many offspring.

As soon as the bride entered the house she made her greeting and threw walnuts and hazelnuts. Everyone then sat down to eat. When the meal was over, a tray with a jug of wine was placed in front of the couple and one by one the relatives filed past them drinking a little wine, wishing them well, and throwing some money into a red scarf laid out on the table. This was done to help out the groom with the expenses of the wedding.

Dimitrios Gigantes - Macherado"

Zakynthos holds a a number of festivals, all of them religious and all of them occassions to observe the joyous spirit of the islanders and to hear the music and songs of Zakynthos.

The special nature of religious celebration on the Ionian islands is deeply rooted in the past. During the period of Venetian occupation, much pressure was exerted on the Ionian islanders to convert to Roman Catholicism. Consequently, the people drew even closer to their own Orthodox faith, thereby strengthening both religious and nationalist tendencies. One result was that they made saints of three of the islanders themselves —St. Dionysios in Zakynthos, St. Gerassimos in Cephalonia and St. Spyridonas in Corfu— who were their own compatriots, sanctified during this period, and with whose relatives they fraternized in the marketplace.

The saint's procession round the town.

The procession in a painting from an earlier

There are still descendants of St. Dionysios on Zakynthos today with the surname Sigouros. In this way they enhanced a feeling of mutual trust and solidarity among all those whose fate it was to suffer the Venetian subjugation.

The islanders were therefore able to strengethen their morale and maintain their resistance to the occupiers. Their Orthodox faith thus became closely connected with political struggle, much as it had throughout most of Greece during the Ottoman occupation. And over the years, religious festivals became the forum for the islanders under Venetian rule.

Today the occupiers are gone but the tradition of religious festivals lives on. St. Dionysios, for example, to whom innumerable festivals were once dedicated on Zakynthos each year, is now celebrated twice-yearly, on 24 August and 17 December, both with austere religious processions and with joyful celebrations accompanied by singing, dancing and firework displays. On the Saint's Day, everyone celebrates and the islanders greet each other with the phrase 'Chronia Polla' meaning 'May you live for many years'. The islanders also maintain a long list of other religious feasts, including St. Lazaros on the afternoon of Easter Sunday; the feast of the Virgin Mary on 15 August; St Kiriakis on 7 June (in the village of Alikana); the feast of the Annunciation on the last Sunday of August (which takes places at the monastery of the same name), that of St Paraskevi on 26 July (at the Volimes). There is also the feast of St. Timotheos and St Mavra at Macherado, St Theotokos Katastarnas (on 15 August in Kalipado), St. Joseph of Samakos (at Gaiitani), and the feast of Zodohos Pigis (in the suburbs of Bohali) and many others.

One of the most beautiful festivals to experience on Zakynthos is the *Easter celebration* which, while corresponding in most ways to the traditions ritually maintained everywhere in Greece, also has a unique flavour all its own.

Easter gets under way on Holy Tuesday when the choir of the cathedral of St. Dionysios chants the traditional *'Kasianis'* psalm. Good Friday customs are perhaps the most unique, with all the able-bodied inhabitants of *'Chora'*, the main town, talking part. Preparations begin in the morning for the procession of the *'epitafios'* — a represenation of Christ's bier, decorated with wildflowers which every church in Greece prepares. It is then carried through towns and villages in every part of the country.

What makes this rite so special in Zakynthos is that the first Good Friday procession, begining exactly at 2 p.m.

...ch processions are a common expression of religious devotion on Zakynthos.

(the hour, according to the bible, when the ordeal of Christ's crucifiction began) follows the figure of Christ on the cross. For centuries now, this procession behind the cross has followed precisely the same route through Zakynthos town, begining at the Church of St. Nicholas of Molos, cutting across St. Mark's Square on the main street and proceeding to the Church of St. Saranta before heading back through Solomos Sqare to end at St. Nicholas church once more.

So important is the continuity of this tradition for the islanders that even the tragic events of 1953 could not deter them. On the first Easter after the earthquake, in fact, when Zakynthos lay in ruins, army bulldozers cleared a path in the rubble along the traditional route so that the procession could take place as usual. In that year, as the Zakynthians made their way with difficulty through the annihilated town, they were lamenting not only the suffering of Christ but the devastation of their land and lives.

After the procession of the cross, the whole town is plunged into mourning. Then, on Good Friday evening, the procession of the *'epitafios'* itself takes place, a ceremony which still echos the grandeur of Zakynthos past. In fact, many of its elements still bear some resemblance to a painting which hangs today in the Zakynthos museum. The picture dates from the peaceful era of Venetian occupation and depicts the procession, just as it is today, making its way through the streets of the town. The only difference is that instead of the school children and boy scouts beating the mournful rhythm on their drums as they do today, there are Venetian drummers, dressed in colourful uniforms. Alongside them are marchers bearing aloft bright flags, the banners of the guilds and the churches which epitomized the islanders' struggle to maintain their identity against the forces which sought to Latinize them. Behind the marchers are the priests with their gold embroidered robes. The painting also reveals the towns Venetian palazzos, many of which remained intact until the 1953 earthquake. The only one still standing today is the church of St. Nicholas of Molos.

Today, during the *'epitafios'* procession, a brass band plays the moving hymn traditionally sung for this occasion — a wonderful piece of music which is also something of a legend.

According to well-documented sources, this impressive composition has been played during the Easter celebrations on Zakynthos since 1700, or even earlier, and is said to have been composed by the Zakynthian Ioannis Planyteros.

Another beautiful and mournful hymn, written by an anonymous Zakynthian —"The Lament of Good Friday"— was once chanted exclusively by women dressed in black, in a number of variations in every village on the island. It is still performed in a few mountain villages today. In this song, Mary, the mother of Christ, speaks with St. John while they keep their vigil at the foot of Christ's cross. In it is contained the words of a mother's anguish and grief, transformed into a lament for the pain and despair of all humanity, symbolized by the brutal separation of mother and son:

— *"My dear St. John, baptizer of my son, have you not seen my son and your teacher?"*
— *"Who has a mouth to tell, a tongue to clarify, a palm large enough to show you your son?"*
— *"You have a mouth to tell me; a tongue to clarify and a palm large enough to show me my son."*
— *"You see that naked body who is on the holy wood...*
  Who wears a shirt covered in blood...
  Who wears on his head the nails which they will hammer into him...
  Who offers them the bile with which they will cover him...
  That is your son and my teacher."
— *"Oh where is a cliff I can leap from for my only son?"*

And here follow the pained words of a mother who has lost a son, words filled with human anguish and the despair brought by the brutal separation of mother and child.

Another Zakynthian Good Friday custom unique in all of Greece is the *'mandsies'* — practical jokes which the islanders are free to indulge in beginning on the night of Good Friday until dawn on Saturday, when the mass is held. The most well-known of these pranks, still played today, although much more low-key, is switching shop sings. When all the shops are shut, groups of Zakynthians dash through the town taking down signs and changing them around. On Saturday morning the shopkeepers arriving to open up for the day find completely different signs hanging over their stores. Above the Pharmacy might hang the sign: FERTILIZERS -ANIMAL FODDER or above a Jewelry shop: IRON RODS.

The origins of this unique custom, played out for centuries now, cannot be verified. One opinion is that it began as a vindictive act against Jewish merchants who at some point during the Venetian occupation settled on Zakynthos and dominated the commercial life of the town. There was still a significant population of Jews on Zakynthos until the time of World War II. Today this custom, along with many others, has faded and is slowly dying out.

On Saturday night at midnight, after mass, (the ritual of Jerusalem is followed), the melodious bells of the cathedral begin chiming. It is the joyful signal to begin rejoicing to commemorate the Resurrection of Christ. The band strolls through the streets of the town playing traditional music and the entire island celebrates late into the night. On Easter Sunday afternoon families gather to feast, sing and dance and to celebrate one of the island's most joyful feasts.

Works by N. Kantounis.

Zakynthos, at the crossroads of East and West, has felt the aftershocks of the powerful movements of history in every era. A sudden economic boom, based on agriculture and trade and on the formation of craft guilds in the 17th century permitted a flourishing of the arts on the island. And when the Ottoman Turks overran the island of Crete, many Creten artists immigrated to Zakynthos and played a significant role in shaping the art and technique of icon painting (hagiography) there.

The Zakynthian historian Zois makes reference to *'various styles of Cretan reformation of the austere Byzantine icon.'* In post-Byzantine icon paintings, egg washes were used on wood. This technique is a blend of Byzantine and Renaissance methods and the tradition began on Zakyn-thos when the Cretan icon painter **Michael Damaskinos** spent some time there towards the end of the 16th century. The tradition continued with the work of **Elias Moschos** (1649-1686) and **D.** and **G. Moschos**.

Painting in Zakynthos was also tied to the Ionian school of naturalistic art, heavily influenced by the Italian Renaissance. It expressed the social and ideological characteristics of the new ascending force on the island — the bourgeosie. With the 18th century came a real break with the Byzantine tradition which paved the way for the icon painters **Panayiotis Doxaras, Geronimos Stratis Plakotos, Nicholaos Doxaras, N. Koutouzis and N. Kandounis** etc. These artists decorated Zakynthian churches with watercolors, metal engravings and wood carvings.

In the Ionian School, the saints are depicted realistically and not mysteriously or metaphysically. Their preference was for lively, joyful figures. They also often included scenes from the daily life of the islanders in the countryside. Disdaining the exaggerated passion and intense theatricality of Byzantine tradition, they moved instead within the framework of a disciplined art, moderated by faithfullness to original movements and forms yet reflecting the ancient traditions of restrained grandeur and a perfect equilibrium of forces, not only in the rendering of their subjects but in their understanding of matter itself.

Other painters of the 19th century, including **A.** and **G. Griparis, K. Giatras** and **D. Tsokos**, carried on the tradition, expressing through their icon portraits an atmosphere reminiscent of the Zakynthos 'cantades' and of opera, another well-loved musical form on the island. Their portraits, idealizations which reflected the culture of the Renaisance, nevertheless never veered too far from realistic human form and dimension.

Apart from sculptures from antiquity, of which very few have survived on Zakynthos, there are a great many important pieces of carved wood and worked silver. The most important woodcarver on the island was **Yorgos Bafas**, son of the woodcarver and goldsmith, **Diamantis Bafas**. There are today three magnificent pieces by him in the church of St. Dionysios: an icon of the saint, measuring 1.50 m. by 1.20 m., a funereal urn, and a reliquary for his hand, decorated with a series of miniatures of rare artistic value.

A Zakynthian icon in carved silver.

The works of other Zakynthian woodcarvers that decorate churches, homes and even furniture is just as significant. This artistic tradition also had its origin in ancient times. Among the best-known artists of this genre, are **Anastasios Vlahos**, the brothers **Andravidiotis** and **Antonio Kourelis** and others.

The Zakynthos artist Stephanos Xenopoulos (the brother of the writer Grigorios) gained international fame and recognition mainly for his work in mosaics — a art dating back to prehistoric times. A Cartoonist and caricaturist at the start of his career, Xenopoulos later studied art in France and dedicated himself to mosaicking. Many significant works of his can be found in museums and churches throughout Greece and in a number of other countries as well.

The carved wooden and gilt screen of St Demetrius 'Kolla' (1690).

It is in the churches of Zakynthos that one can see the splendid inter-relation of the work of the island's gifted painters, sculptors, wood-carvers, and gold and silversmiths. The churches differed and are still different from the churches in the rest of Greece, although they are similar to those on the other Ionian islands. There is not one of the Byzantine style. Due to the influence of the West, the main building of these churches is long and low with the number of vaults varying according to how large the church is.

There are also differences in the interior decoration which is mostly influenced by Western and not Byzantine technique. There is a very secular flavour in the interiors. The women's quarters are such that one imagines one is looking at the balcony of a theatre or opera house. Thus one does not does not have the feeling of being in a place of worship.

Today the greatest pride of the Zakynthos churches is their decorative wood carvings and silver work. Even the churches that were built after the earthquake still have their carved altar-screens. The main church of Volimes was even rebuilt around it's remaining altar screen. In the town some of the finest churches are St. Triada, on the road to Krioneri, St. Lazaros on the other side of town and Our Lady of the Angels near the Hotel Xenia.

St Nicholas at Kiliomeno.

An essential but differentiating characteristic of every church is its belltower. It stands as a kind of symbol, the pride and boast of its parishoners. The tunes that the bells ring out are easily recognized by the inhabitants. Of course, the musical sensibilities of the Zakynthians is well known.

Bell towers on the Ionion islands are built to daring heights. Their melodies, echoing off the stones, rise to a crescendo, elevating them still higher. Their irrational height challenges the levelling force of earth-quakes. They reach up into the sky expressing goldliness but they have their base in the earth. Like the spirit leaving the bondage of earthly matter, they dare the destructive forces of nature.

The church of St Paraskevi at Meses Volimes, showing the carved wooden screen.

Another exceptional folklorist element of Zakynthos culture is the popular theatre. This local tradition took shape during the period of the Venetian domination and its origins are connected with the popular Italian theatre of the Middle Ages and Renaissance.

The presence of the Italians on the island and the transplantation of elements of their social and cultural life helped the Zakynthians and the other Ionian islanders from the 16th century onwards to become involved with music and theatre. In 1571, they staged their first performance —"The Persians" by Aeschylus— and there followed comedies and other plays. These plays, however, were only performed in the salons of the aristocrats, and in Italian. In the last year of the Venetian occupation a small theatre was built for performances for the people.

From the mid-19th century on, the passion of the Zakynthians for opera prevailed over the theatrical life of the island. Aristocrats and ordinary people alike threw themselves into the enjoyment of 'bel canto' with all their hearts. Their appreciation of music is such that they can discern the slightest dissonance, and it is said that they have as much disregard for false notes as they have for earthquakes.

Of particular signficance in the island's theatrical tradition are the plays known as 'omilies' - which literally means 'speeches'. They were a form of people's theatre, usually written by an anonymous author so that he could freely satirize social injustice and the personal weaknesses of those in authority.

It is not known whether the 'omilies' were brought to Zakynthos by the Cretan refugees or whether, even before the fall of Crete, this form of Cretan theatre had reached the island. During the Venetian domination, however, the 'omilies' were much in evidence. They were performed by men only, who disguised themselves with masks so that they could not be recognized by the audience. The female roles were played by the more elegant men, wearing shimmering dresses covered with embroidery and sequins. The masks they wore were not made of fabric like those used to portray men's characters. They were specially crafted and used only to portray females. So if one did not look at the feet, (which often betrayed the male player behind the disguise despite the fact that he wore womens pointed shoes), and if one ignored their height, one had the impression of looking at real and even attractive female masqueraders.

The 'omilies' were used as political ammunition, first by the people's movement and later by the Radical party. All the themes capable of moving the people emotionally were woven into the plots. Even when the works revolved around characters such as kings, princes, and princesses, the authors managed to commend the virtues of humility, love, loyality to friends and altruism and to denounce injustice — especially social injustice and the greed and avarice of the nobles always had an important place in the 'omilies', which were performed outdoors.

Even today, the 'omilies' performed in the villages are never exclusively a form of entertainment. They are educational as well, aiming to imbue the people with higher spiritual values and to cultivate the high standards traditionally fostered by the Zakynthos civilization.

'Omilies' were not only performed in the village of Zakynthos but also in the 'Chora'. Small groups prepared the plays and performed them, themselves. They chose outdoor venues in flat, open spaces — sometimes on wide cross-roads, especially those close to the public places where the villagers usually gathered. They even performed at the places where villagers met to await their local bus. The members of the groups were fishermen, men from the trawler crews, cart drivers, hawkers, grocers, cobblers and others. In pre-earthquake Zakynthos, the moving force and soul behind the 'omilia' movement in the town was a grocer named Spyros Grigoris. A self-taught man of the people, a good singer of 'cantades', he sold his vegetables all over 'Chora', always with a song. He managed to do his business and simultaneously manage the preparation and performance of the 'omilies'. He was the treasurer of the group and the director of the players. The players themselves made the masks but were helped by other painters, because the masks were such an important feature of the show. The 'omilies' in the 'Chora' were only performed at Carnival time, when the group travelled from one neighborhood to the other with the show and finally performed in St. Mark's Square, where the festival traditionally took place. The play was acted out in the middle of the square, filled to overflowing. Once it was over, the festivities began.

One of the characteristics of Zakynthos' popular theatre is the way in which the local actors view their activity. They do not consider the playing in 'omilies' a professional occupation but rather a part of their lives, something done joyfully, with 'kefi' (which translates as high spirits), a creative way of establishing warm contact with their fellows, to whom they offered their souls in order to entertain them.

The 'omilies', which are still performed today in the villages of Zakynthos, are not restricted to old-fashioned themes. They often deal with contemporary social problems and at times, though the scenario is old, the script is modern. Thus there is continuity between old and new-between the past and the present.

In addition to the 'omilies', there were also amateur theatrical groups who organized performances of ancient and medieval works on the island. The historian Spyridon De Viazis notes one of these — "The Persians" by Aeschuylus, in Italian.

There were a number of historical theatres on Zakynthos, inclunding The Theatre of the Patriots, built in 1813, where Ugo Foscolo's "Atreus and Thiestis" was performed, with music by Ludovico Plastonis. Another, built in 1826, was the venue for, among other plays, "The Royalist", by Matesis and "Hasis" by Gouzelis. There was also the Appolon Theatre, built in 1827. The Foscolo no longer exists. It was a neoclassic building designed by Schiller, one wing of which housed the "Lombardian' casino, a political club of the writer and historian Lombardos — art and politics under the same roof.

An annual theatre festival was established on Zakynthos in 1965 called the "Conference of Medieval Popular Theatre." It takes place each summer, with performances of the Zakynthos 'omilies', and other works of Zakynthian and Cretan theatre, and with the participation of popular theatrical groups from Greece and abroad.

Zakynthos can be considered the most important centre of art in the modern Greek state. Few places in Greece can be compared to the island in terms of its contribution to literature and art. There is hardly a facet of the intellectual and cultural life of the country which does not bear the stamp of a work, or of the influence of at least one Zakynthian talent. Thus the island can be considered the backbone of modern Greek literature.

The first Greek academy was founded on Zakynthos in the 16th century. In 1815, the Academy of the Free Western Islands was established, in 1812 the 'Leschiotis' Academy and in 1829, the Medical Academy.

Zakynthos honours Andreas Calvos.

The statue of Dionysios Solomos, erected after the earthquake in the main sq

...ch bears his name.

The main spiritual guides for these academic enterprises were: **Antonios Martelaos** (1753-1819), the teacher of Foscolo, Kalvos and Solomos; **Antonios Matesis** (1724-1875), a gifted playwright; **Yiorgos Tertsetis** (1800-1875) and **K. Lombardos**, a modern Greek historian. Then there was the Italian-speaking **Ugo Foscolo**, born on Zakynthos in 1778, and the exceptionally distinguished poet **Andreas Kalvos** (1798-1863). The most famous Zakynthian writer, who won both Greek and inernational recognition, was **Dionysios Solomos** (1798-1857), author of the poem "Hymn to Freedom." The first two 4-line stanzas of the poem were set to the music of composer Nicholaos Mandzaros, from Corfu, to become the Greek national anthem:

'I know you by the edge
Of your formidable sword.
I know you by your countenance
which instantly measures the world.

You arose from the bones;
The sacred bones of the Greeks
And valiant as you always were
I salute you; I salute you Freedom."

Notable Zakynthian writers and poets of the 19th century were **I. Tsakasianos, Andreas Martzokis, Andonios Biskinis**, etc. From the recent past, one can single out **Grigoris Xenopoulos** (1867-1951) for his versatility in producing both plays and prose of distinction, as well as for making a significant contribution to children's literature. He especially gained fame after the 1953 earthquake, when his works became the only existing source of rich descriptions of Zakynthian life and traditions.

ERNA MIA TERRA
PRESCRISSE IL FATO
RIMATA SEPOLTURA

The cenotaph of Hugo Foscolo with the sculpture entitled 'Grieving Spirit'.

Despite this dramatic development in tourism, however, the islanders have in general not given up farming the land. On Venetians times raisin production flourished more than the cultivation of olive trees as the yield was more profitable. During these times, two things were punishable with death — treason and raisin smuggling. The Peloponnesians had brought the technique of raisin production with them when they settled on Zakynthos after deserting their homes because of the many Turkish attacks on their land. This production brought wealth to Zakynthos and became the farmer's main source of income. This situation continued until World War II, when the special vines required for raisins were destroyed through the inavailability of sulphur and copper, used as insecticides. After the war the foreign markets for Greek raisins were lost.

used by those responsible for guarding and supervising the fields, providing a cool refuge from the hot sun and heavy work. Nowadays they are sometimes rented out, and some have even been built on beaches for those desiring a simple holiday hut right by the sea.

Industry has never taken hold on Zakynthos and manufacturing is limited mainly to the level of handicrafts.

There are workshops processing farm produce, making putty (stucco) — from the magnesite mined on the island, and plaster of Paris. There are also the traditional workshops making powders, candles and nougat. Zakynthos nougat is very famous, and considered by some the best in the world. The craft of powdermaking is an ancient tradition and has been highly profitable for the island in past eras.

Today the economy depends on the cultivation of olive trees, vines and citrus fruit, which yield the island's main export products — olive oil, wine ('verdea', or local wine), raisins and fruit. Animal breeding and fishing have never developed significantly on Zakynthos.

The type of farming peculiar to Zakynthos (olive groves, citrus orchards and vinyards) promoted the development of an unusual type of architectural construction — the 'vergaki'. These are huts, simply constructed with four corner posts 1.50 -2.00 metres high, usually of cypress wood, dug into the earth. The posts support a skeleton framework on which walls, made from leaves or from sheets of dried came tied together, are fastened. They usually have one floor only with a veranda but have also been built on two and three levels. Originally, the huts were

It is, however, tourism that has developed most dramatically on Zakynthos.

Today the smiling island, with its peaceful life has become much frequented and sought after, especially in the summer when it is host to scores of visitors, both Greeks and foreigners. The roads have changed and been widened and there are no more quaintly cobbled streets. Now the Strada Marina along the wharf is no longer the deserted road it once was, with the occassional idle passerby. It now teems with life and motion. A row of shops stretches from the church of St. Nicholas of Molos to the Church of St. Dionysios, offering every possible kind of souvenir. Cafeterias, Pizzarias and every other type of restaurant arrange their chairs on the pavements and on the wharf. It is always crowded with foreign visitors, who come in waves with the ferryboats from Kilini.

Bicycles and carriages, picturesque notes in the life of the town.

Tourism on Zakynthos has always been a summer phenomenon, though the islanders should aim to extend the season to improve their tourist earnings. Zakynthos' moderate climate is very similar to that of the French Riviera, with abundant days of sunshine and mild winters without snow fall. These factors would lend themselves to a profitable development of winter tourism on the island, similar to that enjoyed by the French Riviera, were it not for the fact that Zakynthos lacks a suitable infrastructure and cannot offer visitors the same kind of exciting nightlife to be found in Nice or Cannes.

Tourism has sparked a significant development in the sector of summer apparel and handicraft manufacturing, carried on by small workshops and cottage industries. The villages of northern Zakynthos are the centre of this industry. At Volimes there is a profitable production of a rich assortment of woven goods, handmade lacework and embroideries, kilims, and other touristic items for which Zakynthos is justifiably well known.

In 1988, the "Women's Co-op for Country Tourism" was founded at Ano Volimes, in the framework of a national program designed to give women in country districts more opportunity to became involved in the island's tourism.

The cottage industry for the manufacture of woven goods, embroidered lacework, kilims and other touristic items has already spread to many villages on Zakynthos, and in some of them comprises their main source of income. Villagers often display the goods outside their homes, transforming the once strictly farming villages, and sell the bulk of their merchandise directly to passing tourists. The remaining goods find their way into the tourist shops in island.

A TOUR OF THE ISLAND

In the daily life of Zakynthos today one can discern the echoes of a powerful folk tradition. That tradition was brutally interrupted by the earthquake of 1953, and slowly eroded by the new ways of life of the modern age.

The most exciting places are always those you discover by yourself, and not those which a tourist guide tells you to admire.

The guide book can be considered a stimulating starting point for discovering the 'Flower of the Levant'.

The Town of Zakynthos

The town of Zakynthos —known as Chora, apart from its official name— is a new town, lying in a semi-circle between the foot of the Castle hill and the sea. It stands on exactly the same site as did the town which was wrecked by the earthquake and the fire of 1953. The new buildings have attempted to retain the style of those they replace — a mixture of neo-Classical and Venetian, with a strong dash of an entirely local atmosphere.

In antiquity, the settlement here stood higher up, on the flat top of Castle hill. This was one of the very few positions on which it was actually possible to build a town: the west coast of the island is rocky, while the shallow, unprotected bays in the south were unsuitable as anchorages.

The town and the harbour; the Ayios Haralambos river can be seen.

Here on the east coast, however, the sheltered sandy bay beneath its steep hill formed a natural refuge from the forces of nature and also a place of strength from which to fight off enemy attacks. So it was on this hill that the ancient acropolis of Psophis was built and on which the Venetian city stood in later times. With the passage of time, the growing population and the changing living conditions caused the city to expand along the strip of ground between the foot of the hill and the sea. Because this strip was narrow, the town stretched out along the shore. Later still, the trade in the new harbour, and commercial activities of the islanders and the continuing growth of the population made necessary the filling in of the shore with earthworks for further expansion: the church of St Nicholas on the Mole (see the town plan) was once on an island, and a bridge linked it to the island. Solomos Square, too, stands on filled land.

The description of Zakynthos which follows was written in about 1930:

The new town of Zakynthos extends in an irregular circle —somewhat amphitheatrical in the centre— across the eastern slopes of the Castle. It has a length of approximately two kilometres and a breadth at its widest point of point of about one and a half. In former times, the town was divided into 14 quarters, which, apart from the Jewish quarter in the centre of the town, took their names from the principal churches. Most of the streets were cobbled, and the main roads had recently been surfaced with asphalt: these included the main street (Megali Rouga, now called Anexartisias St, which runs through the centre of almost the whole town and is lined with arcades), Foskolou St and others. The town has two large squares, one named for the poet Solomos, planted with trees and containing the municipal theatre and the Lomvardos political society, and Dimokratias Square, once called Ayiou Markou, a famous and historic place which is the site of the Catholic cathedral of St Mark, one of the finest in the East, the municipal clock, the Byzantine Museum and the magnificent Zakynthos Club.

Another square with trees is to be found in the southern part of the town, and there are other smaller squares or open areas in front of some of the churches. Tavoulari St runs from Solomou Square to Dimokratias Square: on it is the fine church of All Saints with its bell-tower, in front of which, on a marble plinth, is the copper bust of Maitland, first British Commissioner under the Protectorate, with a scene in relief by the Danish sculptor Thorvardsen; also on this street are the Landowners' Club and the Pawnshop, beneath which is the archive building, dating from 1670.

The town has a number of outstanding buildings, including the Koumoutos mansion, the Romas mansion —which houses the Prefecture— the Nana D. Lountzi mansion, the Ioannis D. Lountzis mansion, the Ambeloravdis mansion, the Martinegos Gaitas mansion (currently an old people's home), the Michalitsis mansion (with the courtroom) and the artistic mansion which once belonged to the Savvatos family, in the Italian style, which was used as a seminary in Venetian times. The following are the most important of the many churches of historical and artistic interest:

Our Lady 'Faneromeni', built in 1300 and reconstructed in 1633, of interest for its paintings and, in general, its art-work, with icons by the famous painters Doxaras, Tzanes, Victor Moschos, Plakotos, Nomikos and others and a wonderful carved wooden screen; the Cathedral, next to which a nunnery has stood since 1680; the Holy Trinity; All Saints, with icons by Kantounis and Moschos; Our Lady "Evangelistria', with icons by Koutouzis and Kantounis, St Spyridon 'Flambouriaris'; Our Lady of the Angels, with an artistic plastered facade, and St Dionysios, with the larnax containing the relic of the island's patron saint, Dionysios.

In the northern part of the town is the Catholic church of Santa Maria, where in 1544 a plaque inscribed by Cicero came to light and which contains the tomb of the Philhellene Gys. There are bell-towers at the churches of St Dionysios, Our Lady 'Faneromeni', Our Lady 'Hodeghetria', Our Lady 'Pikridiotissa', All Saints, St Mark and the Holy Trinity. The esplanade —officially known as Lomvardou St but usually called the Strata Marina— stretches from Solomou Square to the church of St Dionysios, and, with its fine buildings and broad pavements on both sides, is one of the most outstanding streets of its kind in Greece. In front of it lies the harbour, protected by a breakwater 700 metres in length.

The town of Zakynthos and the castle, as seen f

Near the dock is a marble column erected in memory of the Zakynthians who fell at Gribovo in the war of 1897. From the town, Filikon St leads to the historic church of St George 'of the Catholics', where the members of the Society of Friends took their oath, and to Strani Hill, where the poet Solomos wrote his 'Hymn to Liberty'.

Of course, that description of Zakynthos town bears little resemblance to what we see today. The terrific earthquake of 1953 changed the face of the town, but thanks to the efforts of conservationists much of its character has remained and there is ample evidence for comparison of the old and the new.

The efforts to conserve as much as possible of the old form of the town have involved not only its architectural aspect, but also its town planning fabric. It could be said that the layout of the town is roughly the same as it was before the earthquake. There is a long esplanade, the Strata Marina, behind which is the main street, once called the 'Plateia Rouga' and now known as Alexandrou Roma St. Because of the hill which rears up behind it, there are few streets running parallel to the seafront, but those which are at right angles to it are of particular interest. To the north and south, the town embraces the foot of the hill. Most of the building which is being done today takes place in the southern part of the town.

1t Skopos; to the left, the fertile plain of the island.

THE TOWN
OF ZAKYNTHOS

1. Statue of Solomos
2. St Nikols on the Molos
3. Library
4. Museum
5. Telecommunications
6. Church of St. Mark
7. Solomos Museum
8. Church of 'Our Lady of the Angels'
9. Statue of St Pavlou

10. The old center Giofiri
11. Church of Our Lady 'Faneromeni'
12. Church of St Dionyssios
13. Church of Our Lady 'Zoodochou Pigi'
14. Statue of Foskolos
15. Town Hall
16. National Bank
17. Commercial Bank
18. Post Office - Port Office
19. Agricultural Bank
20. Olympic Shopping Centre
21. Statue of Vezal
22. Cathedral
23. Ionian Bank
24. Secondary School
25. General Administration Building
26. Courtrooms
27. 'Pikriditissa' Our Lady
28. Foskolos Shrein
29. Church of the Ascension
30. Hospital
31. Police

Map labels

27

13

ΠΑΦΛΕΣΣΑ · ΑΡΓΙΡΟΠΟΥΛΟΥ · Π. ΚΑΠΠΕΡ

TERTSETI

ALEX ROMA (Rougas Square)

ANAST. LOUTZI

CHR. DAMTRI

DALVANI

N. KENTOU

(STRATA MARINA)

MAKRI

IGNATIOU

K. ZEZA

EL. VENIZELOU

DESSILAS

FILIOPRI

KARVELA

LEONIDA ZOI

PIKI-PRI

OTHAKYSSIOU

D. KOUMANI

ON. KOLIVA

PIKI-PRINI-TSARI

KONSTANTINOU

A. MATESSI

THERIANOU

G. VENDOTI

FILIKION

KASTRO-LOFOS STANI

ARCHIERON

KAPPER

DELAZZI

ROMA

LOUKA KAPPER

KAPODISTRIOU

AGIOU PAITON

ARCHIER-LATA

DIONYSSIOU

GEORGIOU B'

AGIOU MARKOU SQ. (Platiforos)

MAZZAROU

AKROPOLEOS

26

25

24

10

19

17

18

16

15

14

1

2

3

21

4

5

20

22

8

6

7

SOLOMOU SQ.

VEZAL SQ.

We shall begin our tour of the town in **Solomou Square 1**, which we reach from the central dock of the harbour. This is the town's largest square and is also its most recent, having been built —as we saw above— by landfill. Its lines of trees and pretty flowerbeds make it an attractive open space surrounded by aristocratic single — and two-storey buildings and with a state of Solomos, the national poet of Greece, in the centre; In the evening, this is where people congregate for the 'volta', the stroll which is a Greek provincial custom. New friendships are made and old ones renewed as the people of the town enjoy the cool of the evening.

Here in Solomou Square is the church of **St Nicholas 'on the Mole' 2**, the only Venetian building to have survived the fire and to have been restored —externally— to its original form. For many years it belonged to the guild of sailors (each guild had its own banner and its church, whose saint was its patron). St Dionysios served as parish priest here when he came to Zakynthos from Aigina, and some of his ecclesiastical vestments have been preserved in the church.

At mid-day on Good Friday, the procession with the bier of Christ sets out from St Nicholas (see p. 46). Next to the church is the **Municipal Library 3.**

Also in Solomou Square is the impressive building which houses the **Museum of Byzantine Art 4.** This is well worth visiting; the route around the collection leads from the entrance to the right, up to the upper storey and along the whole building before descending once again.

Solomou Square, with St Nicholas 'on the mole' and the Library.

The gallaries of the Museum give some idea of the artistic achierements of Zakynthos.

The Museum's rich collection of portable icons gives a very informative panorama of the local tradition in ecclesiastical painting, with works dating from Byzantine times to the 19th century and approximately one thousand post-Byzantine works in the Ionian and Zakynthian styles. Among the painters whose works can be seen are Damaskinos, Tzanes, Kallergis, Doxaras, Koutouzis and Tsonis. The earlier exhibits (some of them superb) are typical of the Byzantine style of icon-painting, while the works of Panayiotis Doxaras (1622-1700), who studied in Venice, are naturalistic and form the backbone of the Ionian School. This tradition was continued by Doxaras' son Nikolaos and by Nikolaos Koutouzis (1741-1813), whose works can be seen in the church of St Dionysios as well as in the Museum. This collection also houses the screens from the churches of the Pantokrator and St Demetrius, together with the exterior of the little church of St Andrew at Volimes. There are also Hellenistic and Byzantine sculptures and statues.

Solomou Square and Vasileos Yeorgiou II St make up the social centre of the town.

Our Lady 'Pikridiotissa' from Solomou Square.

Vasileos Georgiou II St leads north from the Museum. On it stand the offices of the telephone company (OTE, 5) and Olympic Airways.

The street soon leads to **Ayiou Markou Square**, known as 'Platyforos' by the locals. This triangular square, with its cobbles, is a historic place: it is where the higher social classes of old Zakynthos gathered, and it is the town's oldest 'official' square. Here, in 1797, the 'popolari' burned the hated Libro d'Oro, the 'golden book' in which the names of the aristocrary were inscribed, after what they believed was liberation from Venice by the French. In Ayiou Markou Square was the 'romianiko kazino', or Liberal Club. Today, as we enter the square, the **Catholic Cathedral** 6 stands on our right (the large Catholic population of Zakynthos is a reminder of Venetian times). On the

Ayiou Markou Square contains the Solomos Museum and the Catholic church.

left is the **Museum of Solomos and Eminent Zakynthians 7** (it would be more accurately called the Solomos and Calvos Mausoleum). This interesting museum (to which there is an informative guidebook, in Greek) contains, on the ground floor, the imposing tombs of Dionysios Solomos 1798-1857) and the other great poet of Zakynthos, Andreas Calvos (1792-1869). In the entrance hall is a piece of the tree in whose shade, on Strani hill, Solomos is reputed to have written his 'Hymn to Liberty', which later became the Greek National Anthem, and his 'The Free Besieged', composed in May 1823 to the distant sound of the Turkish cannon bombarding heroic Messolonghi. The tree stood on Strani hill until 1964, when old age overcame it; but today fresh shoots can be seen to have emerged from its roots.

The rooms on the upper floor of the museum contain memorabilia of the great poet and of other eminent men of letters of Zakynthos, together with various collections which have been donated to the Museum.

To the north east of Ayiou Markou Square, in *Louka Karrer St*, is the **Church of Our Lady of the Angels 8** (strictly speaking, of the Presentation of Our Lady). This building was damaged by the earthquake but not totally flattened, and as a result it was possible to rebuild it in the original Spanish 'plataresco' style, with fine friezes of Our Lady and the angels on the exterior and, inside, an admirable screen and wonderful icons by Panayiotis Doxaras and a number of painters in the Cretan style whose names have not come down to us. The church was first built in 1687 and was the headquarters of the guild of notaries.

The street which leads out of Ayiou Markou Square is initially called 21 May St and then continues as **Alexandrou Roma St**: this is the 'Megali Rouga', the main street of the town, as it always has been. For centuries the commercial centre of Chora has been here, and the street owed its importance to its position in the heart of the town and to its arcades on the ground floor of the buildings and up the side-streets. There was a dense market area at either end of the street: the *Yiofiri*, whose customers were chiefly the townspeople, and *Ayios Pavlos 9*, which traded with villagers entering and leaving the town. Today, the street is a lively, bustling place containing most of the town's principal shops.

D. Solomos, from the Museum entrance.
The start of the 'Platyforos' (Alexandrou Roma St), from Ayiou Markou Square.

From Ayiou Pavlou Square we turn towards the sea-front. On our right, two blocks back from the esplanade, is the triangular **Faneromenis Square 11;** the church of Our Lady 'Faneromeni', which gave the sqare its name, was burned down in the fire of 1953.

Of course, the church was rebuilt together with its belfry, and today it looks just as it used to from the outside; inside, however, its artistic treasures have gone. A very few icons of the many important art-works it contained were saved and can be seen in the Museum of Byzantine Art. Faneromenis Square differed from Ayiou Markou Square in that it was the meeting-place for the ordinary people of the town.

We continue in the direction of the esplanade, coming to the Park and the sea-front avenue called the Strata Marina.

The **Strata Marina** is the town's second most important street; it starts in Solomou Square and runs as far as the church of St Dionysios, patron saint of the island 12. In earlier times it was a commercial area, being particularly important for the wholesale trade, and along it stood the warehouses where black currants were stored for export and where important goods were kept. Today, it is still Chora's busiest street, with crowds of people at almost all hours of the day and night: travellers disembarking from the ferries, visitors looking in the windows of the souvenir

The esplanade (Strata Marina).

shops, local people continuing the evening stroll which began in Solomou Square, and people of all kinds eating and drinking in the attractive bars and restaurants. Numerous alleyways (known in the Ionian Islands as 'kantounia') lead at right angles from the Strata Marina back to the Plateia Rouga and the other parallel, streets, thus creating a dense network of roads giving access to all parts of the town; but one is never in danger of getting lost, since the sea can always be seen at the end of the street. On the Strata Marina are most of the *travel agencies* which organise trips to various parts of the island and boat rides right around it. The street also contains the *ferry boat ticket agency* and the *bus station*.

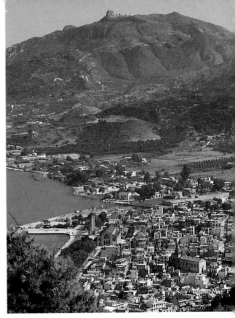

Our Lady 'Faneromeni' and St Dionysios.

The southern end of the Strata Marina is dominated by the large **Church of St Dionysios 12.**

St Dionysios is the patron saint of the island and many of its boys bear his name. He lived in the late 16th and early 17th centuries, and is known principally for his charitable works. He began his monastic life on the isolated Strophades islands, to the south of Zakynthos, and later, when he found himself in Athens on his way to the Holy Land, was ordained Bishop of Aegina. However, a sick man and wishing to return to the monastic life, he resigned from office and retired to the Anafonitria Monastery in the north of the island (see Route 4, page 124).

Inside St Dionysios.

The belfry of St Dionysios by night.

The carved silver larnax of the saint, one of the greatest Greek creations of its type.

His church —one of the three buildings not demolished by the earthquake— is a relatively new building, erected in 1948 to a design by Professor Orlandos. Externally, it is not particularly striking, with the exception of its size and its imposing bell-tower, a copy of that of St Mark in Venice. This bell-tower has become something of a symbol of the island, since it is among the first features which one discerns as one approaches on the ferry. Inside, however, it has superb wall-paintings with scenes from the life of the saint. The church also contains paintings by Nikolaos Koutouzis and Doxaras. The silver larnax in which the relic of the saint is an outstanding piece of work by Diamantis Bafas.

The saint's memory is celebrated on 24 August, the date on which his remains were brought from the Strophades in 1716, for greater safety, and on 17 December, anniversary of his death in 1624. The celebrations on both these occasions are most impressive, and the saint's relics are carried in procession round the town.

This brief walk around the town is, of course, only a first acquaintance. Although the town of Zakynthos is not old, it is an attractive place and one can spend many happy hours exploring its alleys. And although we have described the principal monuments and public buildings above, there is much more still to discover.

The impressive procession of St Dionysios, patron saint of the island.

The town, with the castle hill and Our Lady 'Pikridiotissa' to the right, between them.

The Castle - Bohali

The castle hill, under which Zakynthos town stands, acts as a natural magnet for visitors. On hot summer evenings it is considerably cooler than the town, while at all times of the year it provides superb views. In the winter months, when the heat haze disappears, the coast of the Peloponnese and some of the mountains inland are clearly visible.

A stroll up the Bohali takes about 3/4 hr, in each direction.

We leave from Aghiou Markou Square (see p. 73), following the signpost (right). The road soon begins to climb and, after passing the newly-built Municipal Amphitheatre, we leave the last houses behind.

Soon after this a sharp turning on the left leads to the **Church of St. George 'ton Filikon"** ('of the Society of Friends'). The Society of Friends, formed in the early years of the 19th century, was a secret association of those dedicated to freeing Greece from Turkish rule. It was largely responsible for the preparation of the uprising which turned into the War of Independence of 1821-30, and it numbered among its members some of the most eminent men of the day. This church was where the Zakynthian members of the Society were sworn in, including Theodoros Kolokotronis, one of the leading figures in the fight for freedom. Despite the wish of the islanders to be united with Greece, Zakynthos was not incorporated into the new state until some 40 years after its foundation (see p. 31 on History). Apart from its historical associations, however, the church (which we reach by making a right-hand turn soon after leaving the main road) is a pleasant, cool place and worth a visit for that alone.

On the wall inside the church (on the right near the screen) is a list of the members sworn into the Society. On the left as we approach the church gates is the site of the cemetery of the once-numerous Jewish community of Zakynthos, also commemorated by a plaque in Tertseti St where the synagogue stood prior to the earthquake.

We continue up the hill. When the main road ceases to climb there is a crossroads. The turning right leads up to **Strani Hill**, a pleasant wooded place with extremely important historical associations for Greece. It was here, under the trees, that the national poet Dionysios Solomos would walk, from his mansion which stood in the same area. Indeed it is said that here he wrote the *Hymn to Liberty* which, set to music by Nikolaos Mantzaris, became the Greek national anthem. The spot where Solomos wrote the poem is now marked by a bust of him. The site of the poet's mansion is a little further along the hill-top; it was here, listening to the cannon-fire from the siege of Messolonghi, where Byron met his end, that he wrote his *The Free Besieged*, one of the greatest and most inspiring modern Greek poems.

This road continues down to Akrotiri (see Route 3, p. 114), through a pretty olive forest. This slope was where the houses of the rich were in bygone days; the reason for choosing the site seems to have been because the north winds kept it less damp and unhealthy than the town itself then was.

Returning to the junction, we turn left, following the signpost to Bohali. The road runs between trees and oc-casional houses with gardens and courtyards full of flowers and soon reaches **Bohali**, where it ends. On the way up we pass the Bohali cametery, which according to tradition, was where the Venetians held horse-races and where the ancient Stadium stood. The archaeological finds made here also suggest that there were temples to Apollo and Artemis.

The town and vici

Bohali's main beauty, apart from its charming houses and gardens, is its terrace overlooking the town and the south-eastern part of the island, with the mainland coast in the background.

There are cafes and restaurants, most of which also have live traditional music in the evenings. The church of **Our Lady 'Chrysopiyi'** ('of the Golden Spring'), which stands here and is visible from much of the town below, has a miraculous icon. One can see little of the faces of the icon today, but historians who saw it before the covering of silver was added testify that it bears, in Byzantine numerals, the date 848 and the signature of the icon-painter Panisalkos.

St Dionysios, from above. In the background, St Haralambos.

The entrance to the castle with venetian lion.

Above Bohali, reached by a cobbled path which is a continuation of the road by which we arrived, is the **Castle** of Zakynthos. A Venetian structure of uncertain date, with fortifications reminiscent of similar castles all over Greece (and particularly of Rethymno in Crete), the fortress is now heavily overgrown with pines, but has even finer views, in all directions, than those which can be obtained from below. We enter through the outer gate, with its lions of St Mark, and then pass through two inner gates before entering the site of what was once medieval Zakynthos. At one time there were four Catholic and eight Orthodox churches here, quite apart from the houses and other buildings, but the earthquake completed the damage that time and neglect had already wrought.

We return to Zakynthos town by the road along which we came.

Bohali and Zakynthos castle.

Introduction to the Tour

Our acquaintance with the town was the beginning of our tour, and a starting-point for getting to know the whole of the island.

We have divided our tour into five itineraries which cover the entire island; there are also branches off to various outlying points. We shall come to know something of the glories of nature and history on this island, and, with luck, something of the personality of its inhabitants.

We shall be seeing everything on Zakynthos, from its azure beaches to the monasteries still alive in its hills, from the ruined mansions of the countryside to the churches which their parishioners have restored, from the imposing sheer cliffs of the west coast to quiet villages with friendly inhabitants.

More specifically:

Route 1
To the south west of the town, we pass through Argasi, on the coast with Mt Skopos rising behind, and reach the beaches of Yerakas and Vasilikos (p. 88).

Route 2
To the south of the town, a drive through vineyards will bring us to long sandy beach of Laganas and the cliffs of Keri (p. 96).

Route 3
To the north of the town, a drive throgh beaches of Planos, Tsilivi will bring us to the Alykes (p. 112).

Route 4
We head north and then west, into the upland parts of Zakynthos with their monasteries, and to the steep cliffs of the west coast (p. 118).

Route 5
This is the second half of the trip begun in Route 3, ending on the nor-thernmost tip of the island with its 'blue caves' (p. 138).

ROUTE ONE

Zakynthos (Chora)
Argassi - Vasilikos
Yerakas

This relatively short route, along the southeastern peninsula, takes us through fine scenery to many of the island's best beaches, some of them crowded and some more suitable for those who really want to get away from it all. Care should be taken along the road; though quite well surfaced, it is narrow and busy.

Argasi, close enough to the Chora to be a suburb of

We leave the sea-front and head south, towards the church of St Dionysios (see description of the town).

1.3 km We ignore a turning right to Laganas and the airport (Route two) and cross a bridge over the Aghios Haralambos canal.

The church of St. Haralambos was built in 1729, as an expression of the islanders' gratitude at being delivered from the plague. Over the bridge, we turn left.

e harbour and the belfry can be seen in the background.

The Venetian 'gardiola' (watch-tower).

The beach at Argasi, with one of the huts characteristic of the island.

Our Lady 'Skopiotissa' may have been built on the site of a sanctuary to Artemis.

1.8 km Turning right to Kallitero and Kalamaki, a scattered village at the eastern end of Laganas Bay. We continue straight ahead.

2.8 km We enter the **Argassi** area. This is a verdant valley with Mt Skopos rising in the background. The village, with orchards and abundant greenery, is attractive; it has red-painted houses and straw huts, and vines grow everywhere, covering the walls and shading the courtyards. These traditional features go hand-in-hand with modern tourist facilities and a long safe beach to make Argassi one of the island's most popular resorts. Undoubtedly its proximity to the capital plays some part in this; there is a lot to be said for a resort which is more or less within walking distance of the main town of the island. There are tourist facilities of many kinds. On the last Sunday before Lent there is a carnival here, with folk dancing and feasting.

The ruins of a medieval castle are to be seen near Argassi.

After Argassi, the road turns inland slightly and climbs a little. Here, just before the sign 'Vasilikos', a track turns off to the right. This runs up to a quarry from which a path ascends in about 45 minutes to Mount Skopos (485 m.), passing the ruined monastery of Our Lady 'Skopiotissa' (of Skopos), rebuilt in 1624. In the past, the icon of Our Lady kept in the monastery was brought down from the mountain whenever the island was threatened by plague or pirates, so that the Virgin might protect her flock. Today only the church remains, and is visible from Zakynthos town. On clear days there is an excellent view from the top of the mountain.

The main road continues at some distance from the sea. Here, as at other points on the island, the vegetation consists largely of cypresses growing in among other trees — a combination which is one of the principal features of the Ionian Island landscape and is indeed on of its chief beauties.

Although we have theoretically entered the village of **Vasilikos**, visitors expecting to see a concentrated settlement will be disappointed. As elsewhere on Zakynthos, Vasilikos is more of a concept than a place. The houses are spread over a vonsiderable area, in among the greenery; the fields and orchards are watered by the abundant streams and there are many good beaches.

8.9 km A rough track climbs sharply up on the right (signposted Dafni). Fork right on to the cement track as it ascends and then, at the top of the hill, continue straight for **Dafni** (3.2 km from the main road). This is a beautiful unspoiled beach (minimal facilities), facing the islet of Pelouzo in Laganas Bay. However, restrictions apply to the beach because the turtles use it for nesting (see p. 95). The right-hand fork at the top of the hill goes to the beach at **Sekania**.

10.5 km Rurning (left) for **Porto Zoro** (500 m). The steep track brings us down to a most attractive little beach (tavernas, rooms), effectively the first in a series of bays and beaches which stretch from here to the end of the peninsula.

11.2 km Another turning for Porto

The beach and the rocks at Porto Zoro.

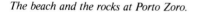

Zoro. From here on the road runs through a pretty pine-wood; there are lots of tracks running down to beaches which have been developed to various extents. Explore them — it's worth it!

13.4 km Turning (left) for **Ayios Nikolaos** (900 metres), a small settlement of cafes and hotels behind a long sandy beach which, however, has little shade to offer.

14.8 km The surfaced road ends at a crossroads. The turning left leads (1.3 kilometre) to **Porto Roma**, one of the island's most popular and attractive beaches, with vegetation running down to the crystal-clear water.

St Nicholas, Vasilikos.

At Porto Roma, the greenery runs down to the beach.

The branch which runs straight on goes to **Yerakas** (1.3 km). Apart from being an excellent beach in a spectacular setting, with a rocky cape protecting it from the south, Yerakas is also a nesting-ground for the loggerhead turtle (*Caretta caretta*) and so there are severe restrictions on both the development of the area and the activities of individual tourists.

The loggerhead turtle used to be common throughout the Mediterranean, but the depredations of man have reduced its numbers to the point where it is now an endangered species. That makes it all the more important that breeding-grounds such as the southern beaches of Zakynthos be protected. The information booths at Laganas and Yerakas will provide more detailed information about the turtles and the ways in which visitors can help them, but in brief:

1. It is strictly forbidden to remain on the beach after sunset. Turtles emerge from the sea to lay their eggs in the hours of darkness.
2. Do not dig in the sand, especially in the upper parts of the beach.
3. Do not use umbrellas which have to be stuck into the sand.
4. Do not take vehicles on to the beach and do not allow dogs to dig there.

In the early summer, when the turtles come up to nest on the beach, their tracks are very clearly visible: grooves in the sand made by their paddles as they force their heavy and unwieldy bodies from the sea to the top of the beach and back again.

The Caretta caretta *turtle.*

Yerakas Bay is one of the prettiest spots on the island.

ROUTE TWO

Zakynthos (Chora) Laganas - Keri

This route takes us to the longest and most popular beach on Zakynthos and also explores a corner of the island which is much less frequented. The return routes proposed lead us back to the town across the heart of the plain which throughout the recent history of Zakynthos has been the source of its wealth.

We start, as usual, from the quay and head south as in Route One.

1.3 km At the bridge we turn right (signpost). It is, of course, also possible to head along the Argassi road and very soon fork right so as to reach the sea at **Kalamaki** and **Ipsolithos**, an excellent sandy beach with clear water. Argillaceous rocks glisten in the most unlikely positions in the crystal-clear water. People cut thick pieces off these rocks and use them to make picture-frames.

Shortly after Ipsolithos to the south, along the waterside (reached only by path) is the huge rock known as the **Vrontolithos**. At its foot is a large cave, open towards the sea. The water of a small spring emerges from the cave and runs down the rock. Further up, another spring creates something similar to a little waterfall. The noise made by this water and by the wind as it whistles round the rock caused the local people to believe that this place was inhabited by the devil. There is a fine sandy beach with azure water: an invitation to swim.

1.6 km At a four-way crossroads (care necessary) we turn left.

1.8 km We enter the Ambelokipi area. One of the features which will soon strike visitors to the southern part of Zakynthos is that the signposts for villages seem to have very little to do which the actual position of the villages themselves: the fact that there is a signpost does not usually mean that one then enters an identifiable main street. The reason for this is that after the earthquake the inhabitants of the villages on the plain thought it more convenient to rebuild their houses on or near their farms rather than on their original sites further up the hill.

Kalamaki, with Laganas behind.

So the villages as such more or less ceased to exist. This is why we use the 'area' when describing these places.

This reversal to living on the farm is, however, from one point of view a continuation of an old tradition. It used to be the case that when one of a family's children got married, a house would be built for the young couple in a corner of the family fields; in this way 'family villages' grew up. That is also why many of the villages bear names which are derived from family names. This process of the sub - division of property is still happening today, so perhaps in a generation or two the villages will have re - formed elsewhere.

3.4 km Turning (left) for the airport, which we soon see.

The bay of Laganas with its two islands, one of the island's most beautiful —and also most highly developed— spots opens up before us.

The islands which lie in the bay are called **Pelouzo** and **Marathonisi**, the latter being heavily wooded. Olives, carobs, fig trees and buches lie behind a beach of yellowish sand running down to emerald water. The road continues across the plain.

4.8 km Turning (left) for **Laganas** (4.5 km). The sandy beach of Laganas (at 9 km in longest in Greece). A wide range of sea sports are available. Laganas is a new village, which sprang up purely to serve the growing tourist trade on the fine beach. This is undoubtedly the part of the island to come to for restful holidays, but those who stay at Laganas will find they have to move around a little if they want to see something of the real Greece and the real Zakynthos.

Off the coast at Laganas lies the islet of **Ayios Sostis**. Once the islet was joined to the island itself, and there was a chapel to St Sostis on it. In the earthquake of 1633, the tip of the promontory split off, the islet may have taken its name ('St Saviour') from a Russian captain who

Laganas by night

Cosmopolitan Laganas, with the Mt Skopos behind.

A street in Laganas, with the islet of Ayios Sostis behind.

The pretty islet of Ayios Sostis

survived a shipwreck. Today, it is linked to Zakynthos by a bridge.

The main road, still running at some distance from the sea, enters the Mouzaki area. On the left can be seen the impressive bulk of **Sarakina**, one of the very few Venetian country mansions to have survived the earthquake, though severely damaged by subsequent abandonment. The name of the house comes from the fact at one time the area was a hideout for Saracen pirates.

The rear of the Sarakina mansion.

The imposing Sarakina mansion dominates the surrounding area.

Tsapalia cave, in an area above Mouzaki where there are many caves.

6.7 km Turning (right) to **Mouzaki**, a large village famous for the quality of the water in its well. The history of the villagve dates back to 1521, and it has two interesting old churches: that of Our Lady bears the date 1741 on its carved wooden screen and also has a wooden ceiling, while St Nicholas, the village 'cathedral', was built in 1815.

Another large village, **Pantokratoras**, stands next to —and indeed almost part of— Mouzaki. High on the hillside above the village is the old church of the Saviour; it seems to hang above the houses. The climb up to the church is worth the effort for the view, and alsoto see the treasures inside. On the side, the green plain stretches across to Chora with its castle, while on the other we can see Mt Skopos and the blue fringe of sea at Laganas. The church itself is a plain little basilica; the Byzantine double eagleis carved into the floor, the screen is wooden, and there are old icons and the remains of paintings on the walls. According to local legend, the church was built by a Byzantine Emperor or by the Empress Pulcheria.

Behind the church is an overgrown graveyard, and a little higher up the hill is a pretty well with carved masonry.

8.3 km Another turning (left) to Laganas.

9.7 km Just past another turning for Mouzaki (by which we shall be returning) we enter the Lithakia area.

11.4 km Turning (right) for **Agalas** (4.5 km), an upland village set high above the rocky west coast among pine-woods. The route as far as this village is most attractive. In earlier days, the villagers of Agalas were wood-cutters by trade. Their village was famous for its mushrooms, and for the quantities of snails to be found there in the spring.

After Agalas, this road leads on to Koiliomeno.

11.8 km Turning (right) for Lithakia, a village with old mansions. This has always been among the more prosperous villages of the area, thanks to its fertile fields in the Laganas area. Many of its inhabitants are also fishermen.

Four kilometres from Lithakia is a deep gorge called **Avyssos**, which has a spring whose water is reputedly good for the digestion. A clay path leads to a cliff-top from which the gorge can be seen twisting down as far as the sea.

12 km. A turning, left, for **Porto Koula**, a narrow but attractive pebbly beach.

The Damianou cave at Agalas.

Keri Lake, Porto Naphtha in Venetian times, a unique spot in the south of the island.

St John, Lithakia.

13.1 km The road continues along the flanks of Mt. Skopos or Megalo Vouno (meaning 'big mountain', 423 metres).

16.0 km Turning (left) for **Limni Keriou** (1.1 km). This pretty hamlet lies at the head of the last cove before the rocky Cape Marathia facing Marathonisi. In ancient times, and until very recently, it was known for its natural pitch wells, which were used for caulking ships and which gave it its Venetian name of Porto Naphta. Attempts were made before the War to prospect here for oil, but they did not prove commercially viable and the workings have been abandoned. The wells by the beach have now been dried out but that described by the ancient author Herodotus may still be seen on the way down to the beach (signpost). At first sight, it looks like a pond of clean drinking water. But at the bottom a more careful look will reveal the black pitch lying among the green weeds.

The spring emits gas, and according to the German geographer and traveller Alfred Philippson this was capable of causing explosions. The last recorded explosion was in 1895, and apart from pitch pieces of pumice stone were also blown high into the air.

Limni Keriou has a pleasant beach and cafes, and boat trips are available in approx. 1.15' hours to the caves, rocks, cliffs and little bays which lie all around Cape Marathias.

After the turning for Limni Keriou the road climbs towards the neck of the cape.

16.9 km Turning (left) for **Marathias** (rough track, 2 km). Marathias is an excellent pepple beach (one of the very few on Zakynthos) with deep, clear water. It has a fine view of Marathonisi. The beach is reached by parking at the cafe and following the path (singnposted) down the hill (about 5 minutes). From here, the track continues up the hill to Keri (see below) but is not recommended.

On Cape Marathias are the famous **'Kamares'** or arches, two huge rocks tower out of the crystal-clear sea to form a cove with a strip of tropically white sand at the end of it.

Back on the main road, we continue to climb and the landscape changes as olive trees give way to pines.

The 'Herodotus spring' at Keri Lake, where the tar bubbles up.

Stone arches and caves adorn the steep shore at Keri.
On this page, the Big Arch of Marathia, and on the following page the Small Arch.

20.3 km Keri, a pretty village, built on the north - facing slopes of Cape Marathias. There is an interesting church in the village, to **Our Lady of Keri**. According to the traditions, Our Lady hid the whole island of Zakynthos in a mist to stop it from being spotted by marauding pirates. The church is finely decorated. A track (very narrow in Keri itself and poor beyond) leads in 1.5 km to the lighthouse on the cape (no admittance).

From here there are spectacular views of the rocky west coast of Zakynthos. These cliffs are extremely dangerous; the only real points of access are Ayios Leon and Porto Vromi, much further to the north. These beaches are only accessible by boat, and even then not easily.

The church of Our Lady 'Keriotissa' with its miraculous icon, which, according to the traditions, saved the village from pirates.

The 'Big Mizithra' from the lighthouse at Keri.

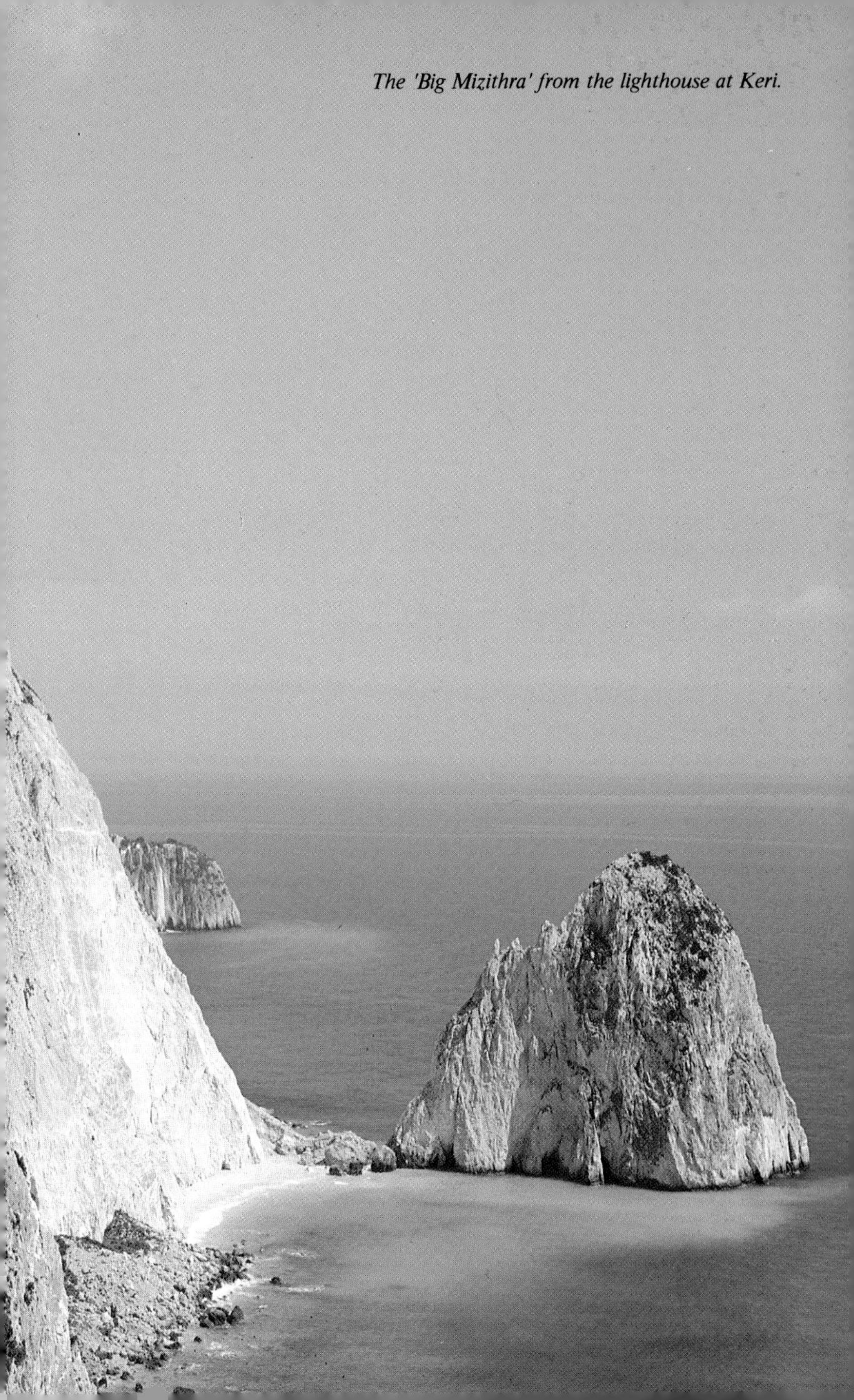

ROUTE THREE

Zakynthos (Chora)
Tsilivi - Alykes

Route Three takes us from Zakynthos town along the coast to the north west, where there are a large number of good, safe beaches. The route we describe runs through pleasant rolling countryside and pretty villages to Alykes and then returns across the plain.

From the seafront, we head north, in the direction of Solomou Square, which we skirt on the side towards the sea.

The 'Voidi' from the Faflas spring.

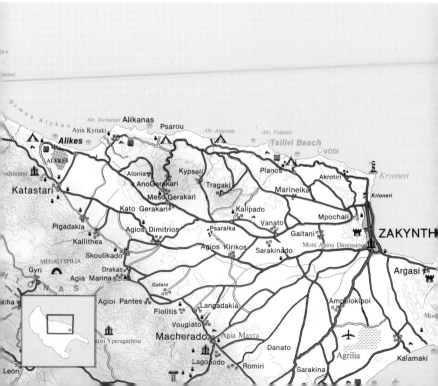

Tsilivi.

0.9 km We enter the suburb of **Kryoneri**, where the NTOG beach is (all facilities, entrance charge). The name Kryoneri ('cold water') comes from a spring from which passing ships used to take on water; the water was also taken into Zakynthos town itself, on donkey-back.

The road continues almost due west near the sea. This is the area which the Greek author Grigoris Xenopoulos (1867 -1951), who was descended from a Zakynthian family, describes in his novel *The Red Rock*. Obviously, a certain amount of literary imagination must have been necessary to turn the area into the memorable setting it becomes in the book.

2.6 km Akrotiri; This is a cool and healthy place among olive trees, one of the closest rural areas to the town. In the pre-earthquake era, the country mansions of the rich were here. We can still see them today, half-hidden in the dence vegetation, but some are ruins and others have been rebuilt in a reminiscence of their former glory.

From here there is an excellent view of the sunset. The rock offshore is known as **'Voidi'** —the Ox— and there are a number of stories as to the reason why. The most common is that the shape of the trees which stood on the rock was reminiscent of the horns of an ox. On the other hand, an old tradition says that once there was a monastery there, linked to the mainland by a bridge. Once a year there was a religious procession to the monastery from the town, led by an ox which was afterwards slaughtered and eaten. Further names for the rock are Fra Filippo, from a hermit who lived there, and Trenta Nova ('thirtynine'), from a number of islanders executed there by the Venetians for demanding more civil rights. The road leaves the shore and climbs in a series of hairpin bends.

3.8 km Turning (left) for Bohali.

5.7 km We emerge from the woods and the beach of Tsilivi opens out beneath us. The blue sea stretches as far as Cape Yidakia (or Todaritis), which ends the curve of the bay.

6.7 km Tsilivi: We turn right for Tsilivi, a long, safe beach with golden sand and shallow, crystal-clear water. Although Tsilivi may not be as long a beach as Laganas, it is cooler in the summer, as the northerly winds blow straight on to it.

7.7 km We turn left, and then immediately right (signposted Yerakari). This is the **Planos** area, once a quiet village but now rapidly developing into a resort area and particularly known for its night —life. The road continues through olive— trees.

9.9 km We turn left, once again following the signs for Yerakari. The branch of the road which goes straight on soon becomes a track. It passes a camp site and provides access to a number of small and quiet beaches (those of Ayios Konstantinos, Kypseli, Tragaki, Mesa Yerakari etc.). Like the corresponding area to the south of Zakynthos town, this whole area is a paradise for those who like to get a little off the beaten track and explore: there are pleasant suprises round every corner:

10.7 km Turnings for the vilages of Marineika and Tragaki, among green hills and dense olive groves.

13.4 km Turning (left) for **Kypseli**, whose new church still has all its old decoration inside, and (right) for Pachi Ammos.

14.3 km Mesa Yerakario: we are now in the midst of the most attractive landscape of rolling hills which bound the plain of Zakynthos to the north-east. At the right time of year, this is a fine place for walkers; the olive groves provide plently of shade, there are old mule-tracks from village to village, and the scenery is very beautiful.

17.0 km The road descends round a series of bends, with the striking bell-tower of the church of St Nicholas on top of Ano Yerakario hill always in front of us.

At the foot of the hill, the road forks; we bear right, and soon join the road from Alykes. The left-hand fork passes though the village of Ano Yerakario (by which we shall return) and then also joins the Alykes road.

21.5 km We come out on to the main road from Zakynthos town and turn right for Alykes.

Tsilivi beach, with its blue sea, lies close to the town.

Collecting salt in the salt-pans.

The long beach at Alykes.

23.4 km As we approach Alykes, there is a turning right for **Alykana**, 2 km the beach at the southern end of Alykes Bay. Mycenean pottery has been found here, and the area is one of the possible sites for the ancient city of Arcadia.

24.5 km Alykes, another of the popular holiday centres on the island; it, Argassi and Laganas are the most highly-developed parts of Zakynthos. A marina is currently under construction at the end of the beach nearest Zakynthos town. The village gets its name from the salt-pans behind the beach. There are abundant fish here, which may be caught by hook, line or spear-gun.

Alikanas, to the south of Alykes.

We return to 21.5 km from the town — that is, to the point at which we joined the main road from Zakynthos town. We turn left. The road passes through the outskirts of Alykes before running out into the countryside once more.

27.6 km After the petrol station, we bear left at the fork (no signpost).

29.5 km We pass through the edge of the village of Kato Yerakario.

31.3 km Kalipado. In the village is a chapel belonging to the Voultsis family, one of the oldest clans on the island. The interior of the church is finely-decorated, and many of the family ancestors are buried beneath the floor, as was for centuries the local custom.

35.2 km As we enter the village of **Vanato**, we turn left. From here, the road runs along the foot of the pretty hill on which the castle stands before ending in Zakynthos town.

The road and the jetty at Alykes.

ROUTE FOUR

Chora - Ayios Dimitrios Katastari -Anafonitria Maries - Kampi - Ayios Leon - Kiliomeno Machairado - Skoulikado

This is a longer itinerary than the previous three, covering the west and some of the north of Zakynthos, and, more specifically, the area around Mt Vrachionas.

It is also more of a sight-seeing tour than a swimming excursion, because this side of the island has little to offer in the way of beaches: the coast is far too steep and rocky. However, the scenery is wonderful and there are monasteries and sleepy villages to explore — just the thing for a more adventurous and quite different day out.

To do this, go straight on from Ayiou Markou Sq. along 21 Maiou St and then follow the signs for Volimes. Three kilometres from the town we come to a crossroads: Gaitani to the right, and Machairado (7 km) to the left. We continue straight ahead, passing Sarakinado, and enter **Ayios Kirikos**, an attractive village with pleasant cafes and restaurants.

10 km Ayios Dimitrios: there are traces of a temple of Artemis Opitais in the village. The fact that the main road goes past these villages does not man, of course, that they are not worth visiting. Lying in a line across the lower slopes of the mountain, slightly above the plain, they are among the wealthiest and biggest villages on Zakynthos. Some of them stood even further up the hill before the earthquake and were rebuilt lower down.

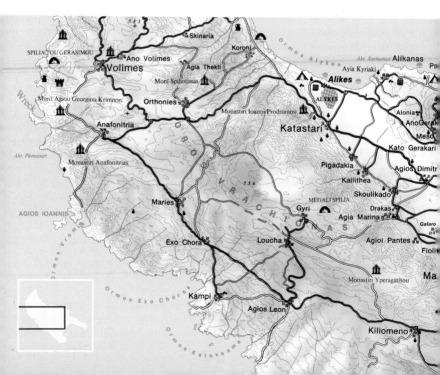

Katastari, the largest village on Zakynthos.

17.0 km Katastari, the largest village on the island and a friendly one.

This village has a peculiarity which is characteristic of Zakynthos. We go first through one half of the village, which is followed by a length of empty road, giving the impression that we have come to the end of Katastari, and suddenly find ourselves in the second half, built amphitheatrically along the roadside. To the left rise the slopes of the mountain, and to the right, below, stretches the lovely bay of Alykes. The church of the Sts Theodori here is worth seeing if only becouse all the ecclesiastical treasures from the surrounding area —from churches, that is, which were destroyed by the earthquake— have been concentrated in it. This is quite a common practice all over the island; one church has been rebuilt and all the icons from the others installed in it.

Alykes bay.

We turn right and begin to climb towards the hilly spine of the island. The road runs initially through olives and cypress trees which we gradually leave behind.

19.0 km Turning (right) for the far end of Alykes beach.

21 km. The road continues to climb and, as we look back, there is a fine view over Alykes, with the plain far in the distance.

We pass on the left a turning to the monastery of John the Baptist, which stands a short way above Hartata, the uppermost part of Katastari, on the lower slopes of Mt Melissa. We do not know when the monastery was first built, but it was renovated in 1617.

The monastery church is a simple basilica flanked by the two-storey

In the courtyard of the Monastery of St John.

The cave in which the icon of Our Lady 'Spiliotissa' was found.

guesthouse building, which has a covered wooden balcony reached by a stone outside staircase. The main entrance is vaulted, with a relief of the Byzantine double-headed eagle; above is the belfry, with four bells. Inside, the church has a good screen, old icons, and the double-heable eagle on the marble floor. Among the monastery's manyh valuable treasures is the icon showing the beheading of John the Baptist, signed "by the hand Theodore Poulakis", a Gospel in a carved silver binding and the monastery codex. John the Baptist was the island's patron saint in the old days, before being suceeded by St Dionysios. In the time of the Tocci, there was a large church to him inside the castle, and later there was a nunnery in his name.

Our road turns west and leaves the coast. We run through a kind of gorge into the centre of the northern part of Zakynthos.

24.0 km Our road turns west and leaves the coast. We run through a kind of gorge into the centre of the northern part of Zakynthos. Soon we come to a crossroads with a turning for **Orthonies** (1 km), a picturesque village with quite a number of old houses.

On our left in the area of the Orthonies crossroads there is a good view of the bare spine of Mt Vrachionas, the highest point on the island (756m).

From Orthonies, the road continues (surfaced, 2 km) to the **Monastery of Our Lady 'Spiliotissa'** ('of the cave'), on the edge of a gorge. Founded in the mid-16th century, the monastery church has a carved wooden screen created by Nikiforos Lambetis in 1712. The foundation gained its name from the fact that the icon of Our Lady in the chapel was discovered in an almost inaccessible cave on the hillside opposite.

The ruinous circular tower of the St George Monastery at Grimna.

After the monastery, the road continues —much rougher— through low hills in the direction of the east coast. This is the **Koroni** area, where the sulphurous **Xingia** spring is located.

26.0 km We fork left for Anafonitria. The other branch of the road leads to Volimes and the extreme north of the island (Route Five). As we approach the top of the western cliffs the landscape becomes more welcoming.

30.0 km Turning (right) for Anafonitria, which we take. After 600m there is a further turning. The right-hand fork leads us into the pretty village of **Anafonitria** (formerly Plemonario) and from there along a rough track (signposted) to the uninhabited **Monastery of St George 'ton krimnon'** ('of the precipices'), in an isolated but magnificent position high above the sea.

It is not known exactly when the monastery was built; it had already been ruined by pirates in 1535 and has been rebuilt several times since then.

The buildings are still in quite good condition today. Inside the plain church, there is a white screen with gold borders; the church also has old icons and, as usual, the double-headed eagle in relief on the floor. A path below the monastery leads to the cave in which St Gerasimos, patron saint of Cephallonia, lived as a hermit.

Returning to the village, we take the other fork. This leads almost immediately to the **Anafonitria Monastery**, from which the village takes its name. A popular place of pilgrimage, this is where St Dionysios spent the last years of his life, and his cell can be seen.

At the entrance to the monastery is a rectangular medieval tower with six macchicolations. Today it is used as a belltower. A vaulted entrance with benches leads into the courtyard in the middle of which stands the church, a simple three-aisled basilica, is the island's oldest. The floor is decorated with a Byzantine double-headed eagle in relief, while faded paintings can be discerned on the walls. The large icon of Our Lady is adorned with gold and silver. The icon of the Virgin was, so the tradition goes, saved from the wreck of a ship which sank off the coast here while fleeing from the fall of Constantinople (1453). The icon was taken to Zakynthos town in times of drought, so that its influence night bring rain. When the rain fell, it was brought back here.

The tower with the machicolations next to the entrance became a belfry; and a general view of the Anafonitria Monastery.

St Dionysios' cell is on the east side of the courtyard. It is a simple, two-storeyed, rectangular building. There are some old icons, and the vestments worn by the saint when conducting the service can be seen.

To the east is the chapel of St Anastasia.

The track continues past the monastery to (7 kilometres) **Porto Vromi**. This is a spectacular trip along and down the precipitous cliffs of the west coast, with exceptional scenery. Care should be taken on the unsurfaced road.

It is difficult to believe that in very ancient times, when what is today the

Porto Vromi, one of the few places on the west coast where the sea is accessible.

plain of Zakynthos was a bog, the island's communications with the outside world, such as they were, took place via these little coves; yet that is what the archaelogists believe.

Down at Porto Vromi, a sheltered cove with swimming off the rocks and from a tiny beach with coarse white sand, where the water is emerald in colour (no refreshments; take water), it is possible to take a boat trip along the coast for a swim and a look at a shipwreck.

Also in the vicinity is **Nisi**, with two fine caves where the show of colours is splendid before returning to Anafonitria.

The beach at shipwreck.

Back on the main road, we head south through pleasant scenery at some distance from the coast.

33 km Maries, a large, upland village swamped in greenery. It has a three-aisled church —rare on the island— dedicated to Mary Magdalene, who reputedly stopped here (her footprint on a rock is shown) and taught Christianity on her way to Rome to protest over the conviction of Christ. The summit of Mt Vrachionas (called Vouni) can be reached from here in about one hour. The views across the whole of Zakynthos and over to Cephallonia are superb.

All the villages along the coast from here southwards have superb sunsets — and cafes strategically placed to make the most of them!

Maries: the old belfry in the square, and part of the village with its typical island houses.

Maries runs down as far as **Stenitis**, a wonderful little cove with greenish-blue crystal-clear water, beneath which mauve or dark-green seaweed can be seen.

36 km Exo Hora, a small village with a fine group of pre-earthquake houses, one of the few such series of buildings to have survived.

37 km Turn (right) for **Kampi** (3 km), a little village on the top of the cliffs. In a little house in the church square of the village is a miniature folk museum. The exhibits were collected by Mr Yakoumelos, a teacher, and are arranged with explanatory notes. They include carved chests, wooden ploughs, distaffs, stone mortars, primitive mechanical equipment, old church icons, wonderful examples of the embroiderer's art and domestic utensils.

At the highest point of the village (Schiza) is an enormous concrete cross, erected in memory of those killed here during the Civil War. Just beneath are some inviting cafes. On the way up to the cross are traces of a (Mycenean?) burial ground. The views along the coast are superb, as is the sunset.

Slightly to the south of Schiza is the so-called **Seal Cliff** ('gremos tis fokias').

According to one version, it got its name from the seals which come to have their pups in the large caves; another story connects the name to the seal-shaped rock at the entrance. The sight is superb: low pine trees run to the edge of the drop, and then the rocks plunge vertically down to the blue waters of Seal Bay.

Stenitis bay, with bluish-green water.

40 km We enter **Aghios Leon**, an attractive white-washed vilage with a church to st Leo dating from the 14th century, and an unusual white belltower. In fact, the structure was originally a windmill, and was converted into a belltower at a later date. The village also has a textile mill run by the State Welfare Organisation, where excellent rugs and woven goods are produced.

40.5 km At the petrol station, a track branches off to the right and runs down across bare slopes to the sea (6 km). It is possible to swim in the little coves with their deep, cool water, but there are no facilities of any kind. A good place for those who want to be really on their own.

After Ayios Leon the road runs through attractive wooded countryside. There is a turning (left) to Loucha and Yiri, the highest villages on the island and among its smallest. The position of **Loucha** is rather strange: as we climb the mountainside, expecting to see it appear in front of us, wee suddenly see it sheltering behind cypress trees at the bottom of a little valley. Perhaps it was built there for fear of pirates. The landscape is strange, too, for Zakynthos: nothing but bare rock. It is reminiscent of the Mani, in the southern Peloponnese, and in fact Maniots did settle here, bringing with them their brand of architecture and their local customs.

Two kilometres further up the hill is **Yiri**, at an altitude of 550 m the island's highest village. To the south is the Hayiotis cave, 65 m in length with some stalactites and Stalagmites: it is largely unexplored.

A Yiros women in the door of her house

45.5 km We pass the turning for the ruined Monastery of Our Lady 'the All-Good".

46.5 km We reach Kiliomeno, the most southerly point on our route. This attractive village, formerly known as **Ayios Nikolaos**, has traditional two-storey houses. It took its earlier name from the large church of St Nicholas, known for its unique bell-tower. This is a tall and imposing structure separated into a number of 'floors' and with little round windows and a fine balcony where the bells hang. It was begun in April 1893, as we are told by an inscription, but never completed: it lacks its top.

After the village the road turns east and runs over the spine of the island once more. Shortly after the village, on a hill to the left of the road, are the scattered remains of Palaiokastro, one of the few ancient sites on Zakynthos. An old Venetian tower can still be seen. The remains are, however, difficult to find. As we descend into the plain there are fine views south to Laganas and east towards Zakynthos town.

We now pass through **Lagopodo**. The village has a fine church to the Saviour, with icons by Grapsas, a carved wooden episcopal throne, a carved and gilded screen and a women's gallery with stone carvings and gold decoation. Between Lagopodo and Machairado is the new and rather fortress-like **nunnery of Our Lady 'Eleftherotria'** ('the liberatrix'). There is a fine view over towards the castle and Mt Skopos.

54 km Machairado, the next-largest village in the plain after Katastari. The principal attraction in Machairado is the church of **St Maura**, which stands on our left as we enter the village. Its bells are highly melodic and it is said that they can be heard almost all over the island. The church itself is a simple basilica, without any particular external features. However, the inside is amazingly richly decorated and contains a number of works of art. The screen is very fine: it is carved in wood and gilded. Note the miracle-working icon of St Maura, with the votive offerings hung about it by the faithful in gratitude for their prayers being answered. The wall-paintings are by Pelekasis, while the ceiling and the pictures were painted by Nikolaos Latsis (see pp. 134-135).

The landscape around Machairado is dominated by the belfry of St Maura.

St Maura.

The Church of the Presentation in the Temple at Machairado.

There are numerous stories about the foundation of the church. One of them relates how the icon of St Maura was found hanging on a fence: the shepherd who found it tried three times to take it to nearby Lagopodo, but each time the icon 'escaped' in the night. In the end, the villagers made up their minds to build a church on the exact point at which the icon was found.

According to another tradition, the saints to whom the church is dedicated (that is, Sts Timotheos and Maura) lived in Thebes, Egypt, where they were martyred in the 3rd century. The icon was brought to the island from Egypt by the Tzavarias family.

The church celebrates its feast day on All Saints' (the first Sunday after Pentecost, usually in June). With the exception of the feasts of St Dionysios in Chora, this is the most impressive ecclesiastical event on the island. It is followed by feasting with traditional music and dance. People from all over the island —and from the mainland, too— come to Machairado for the feast of St Maura.

Machairado also has a church of **The Presentation of Our Lady**, restored by the Archaeological Service. It was built in the 14th century on a rise with a view over the plain to the castle and Mt Skopos. The belfry is highly decorated, and although one of the island's tallest is not a tower-like structure such as that of St Maura. The northern side of the church has fine carvings in relief. Inside, however, it is something of a disappointment, as all the icons have been moved to St Maura. All that is left is the carved marble screen and some marble column capitals, with a relief double-headed eagle on one wall. At one time this was the main church of Machairado.

From the church of St Nicholas at Skoulikado: one of the four paintings showing the miracles of the patron saint of sailors.

A little to the north of this church we come to the pretty village of **Melinado**.

From here it is 10 km across the verdant plain of Zakynthos back to the town. The plain of Zakynthos is very fertile. The currants which were once the island's main and most famous crops are no longer grown extensively: they have given place to other products. There are crops all the year round, and even in the height of summer the plain is an oasis of green. The gate-posts next to the road are all that has remained of the mansions flattened by the earthquake. The positions of the villages can be identified by their belfries, which can be seen protruding from the dense greenery.

We bear left along the 'Riza' road, so-called by the locals because it follows the foot ('riza') of the hills. We pass through **Fioliti**, which took its name from the family which first built it, **Ayii Pantes**, formerly Mikro Galaro, which has a new church to St Marina of outstanding architecture and containing fine works of art, and **Draka** before reaching **Skoulikado**, a typical lowland village.

The name is first mentioned in a document of 1505. There is a musical tradition here, and also a tradition in the folk theatre (principally in 'omilies', see p. 54). These works are of Cretan origin, and the best-known is *Aretokritos*, a local corruption of *Erotokritos*, the famous 17th century Cretan poem.

At the entrance to the village is the proud white-washed chapel of St Nicholas. It has a carved gilt screen, a wooden painted ceiling with the Pantokrator and the 4 apostles, and icons showing miracles worked by the saint. Next to the screen, on the floor, rests a large icon of St Nicholas. It is said that the face of the saint was discovered imprinted on to for it. The frame and the silver were added later to make the rock into an icon. As we climb up into the village, we see the 34 metre bell-tower of the church of Our Lady.

In the centre of the village, in its large square, stands the School of Domestic Science in a new building.

A poor road leads along the hillside from Skoulikado, and after **Kallithea** (or Koukesi), a pretty village with little houses whose courtyards are full of flowers, and **Pigadakia**, another upland settlement dominated by a church of St Barbara to which treasures from an old church of Our Lady 'Vlacherna' and other chapels have been moved, brings us out at Katastari.

A better road turns right to join the main road from Katastari to Zakynthos at Ayios Dimitrios.

At **Gaitani** we bear right and soon return to Zakynthos.

The old belfry at Skoulikado.

The rich decoration of the interior of St Maura at Machairado is reminiscent of the museum-like church of Our Lady 'Faneromeni' in the town, which was knocked down in 1953 (following pages).

ROUTE FIVE

Zakynthos (Chora) Volimes - Korithi - Blue Caves - Ayios Nikolaos Volimes

Route Five is a loop across the outstandingly beautiful and wild extreme north of the island. It starts from the crossroads before Anafonitria described above and thus duplicates Route Four for the first and last 26 km. It would be tempting to think that Routes Four and Five could be combinec and done in a single day, but this would be an extremely long way and would not do justice to the sights of the north of the island. Another possibility would be to do Route Five first, spend the night somewhere in the area and do Route Four the following day.

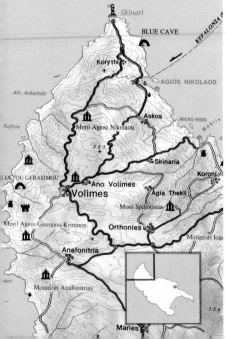

Natural arches at Schinari.

Starting from Zakynthos town, we follow Route Four (see p. 118).

26.0 km At the crossroads at which Route Four turns left for Anafonitria, we bear right. The road climbs gently through attractive farmland.

32.0 km We enter **Volimes**. The village actually consists of three settlements: Kato ('lower) and Mesa ('middle') Volimes, which are more or less united, and **Ano ('upper') Volimes** which stands slightly higher up the hill, which we shall return. They are the centre of life in this part of the island. After the trip from Zakynthos it is a good place to stop for refreshements. Volimes is also famous for its cheese and honey and admire the local handicrafts: Volimes is a major producer of the hand-made lace and rugs for which Zakynthos is justly famous.

Accommodation in Volimes is provided by the Women's Agrotourism Co-operative (office in Ano Volimes), which started life in 1988 as part of a national campaign to involve women in rural areas more actively in tourism and provide visitors with accommodation of a rather different type. Those who wish to gain some experience of what life in the Greek countryside is really like might learn much from a night or two spent here.

The houses of Ano Volimes are built amphitheatrically around the large church of St Demetrius, which dominates in the centre. Ano Volimes

A typical village courtyard at Meses Volimes.

The St Andrew Monastery, whose wall-paintings are at the Museum in the town.

is the island's most typically 'mountain' village.

Meses Volimes has attractive alleyways leading to charming houses with miniature staircases, courtyards and pergolas. In the centre of the village is the large church of St Paraskevi, whose tall bell-tower is an exact copy of that of St Dionysios in Chora.

The church was built in 1633 and renovated in 1700. It has a carved and gilded screen which is a true work of art, and the old ceiling is also in carved wood. The most intersting icons are the large silver works showing St Paraskevi and Our Lady with Christ.

We leave Meses Volimes and pass through Kato Volimes before conti-nuing to the ruined monastery of St Andrew and the dense pine-wood behind it. The view is wonderful from up here, with a little islet visible in the distance below the steep drop.

This islet —which has a chapel to St Andrew on it and caves at sea level— shares the name Diapori with another islet in the vicinity.

35.2 km We cross a rise and an excellent view of the Korthi area opens out beneath us, with Cephallonia in the background. We descend in a number of tight bends.

37.8 km Turning, right, signposted Askos. We fork left.

40.0 km We arrive at a junction, and here have a choice to make if we wish to visit the Blue Caves — about which a preliminary word is perhaps necessary.

Cape Schinari, with its natural arches and blue caves.

The **Blue Caves** are a series of geologocal formations in the cliffs beneath Cape Skinari. Apart from the natural arches produced by erosion, they are remarkable for the colour of the water in the deeper caverns: the refraction of the light makes everything in the water —the rocks and the boat in which we visit the caves— appear an unearthly shade of blue.

A trip to the Caves is highly recommended, not least for the general beauty of the coastline, with its deep, clear sea. The colours are best (in summer) towards midday.

There are, however, three different ways of visiting the Caves. First, by boat from Zakynthos town as part of a trip round the island (details from the travel agencies on the sea-front).

Second, by boat from the lighthouse. We turn left at the junction noted above and a rough track leads in 2.5 km to the end of the cape (cafe), a lonely but beautiful spot. The boat leaves from beneath the lighthouse and reaches the Caves in 10 minutes. Third, by boat from Ayios Nikolaos Bay (see below), which is reached by turning right at the junction. This way, the trip takes about 1 hour.

Whether or not we decide first to make a detour to the lighthouse, we continue (right) for Ayios Nikolaos. The road descends steeply towards the sea.

42 km Ayios Nikolaos is a small bay set stark scenery. The setting is most inviting for a swim and something to eat or drink before con-

inuing. Apart from the boats to the caves (tickets from the booth by the sea, left) there are also occasional car-ferry departures to the south of Cephallonia. Information (and tickets) from the ferry-boat office in Zakynthos town.

Our road continues (unsurfaced for the next 3 km) through **Ayios Nikolaos**.

45.0 km. Turning (left) for **Mega Aloni**, which is one and the same place as the Askos which also appears on signposts.

Along the coast to the south of Ayios Nikolaos is another cave, known as **Xyngia**, in an area in which various underground streams with a high sulphur content pour their waters —and the swimming in the sea where the streams emerge— is much recommended as a treatment for rheumatism, arthritis, etc.

We continue for a further three km before arriving in the Schinaria area, where we join the surfaced road from Volimes. We turn left, in the direction of the sea, and 3 km more brings up to **Mikro Nisi**; here there is a Venetian lookout post built in the 14th century. On its right is **Makrys Yalos**, a golden sandy beach with crystal-clear water.

To the south of Mikro Nisi, after passing Cape Kalamafka, are a series of sulphurous springs. The largest of these is called Xingia, and its waters are believed to be of therapeutic value, being especially recommended for the treatment of arthritis. Xingia cave can be visited by caique from Ayios Nikolaos. Powerful springs well up in the caves, turning the water white and spreading a smell of sulphur everywhere.

We return to Schinaria and continue straight ahead for Volimes.

53.0 km Volimes.

86.0 km Zakynthos.

The little harbour of St Nicholas, with its islet.

STROFADES

The Strofades were known to the ancient Greeks as the "floating islands" because they give the impresion of floating free on the surface of the water. The myth about the winged sons of Boreas gave the islands their name, which derives from the Greek "strofes", meaning "a turning-back". The boys, Kalais and Zitis were out hunting the Harpies, mythical birds with human characteristics who stole the food of Phineas, the King of Xanthi. When they reached this group of islands, they were ordered by Zeus to "turn back". The two sons of Boreas, who were part of the Argonaut expedition lead by Jason, assisted the blind prophet Phineas. He in return gave them invaluable information about the route they should take in their quest for the golden fleece.

A Spartan cup showing the Harpies

There are still "Harpies" inhabiting these islands. They are black, predatory birds, called "artines" by the locals, that feed on fish and whatever else they can forage. Their cry is almost human.

An engraving of the Strophades, from Salvator's book on Zakynthos.

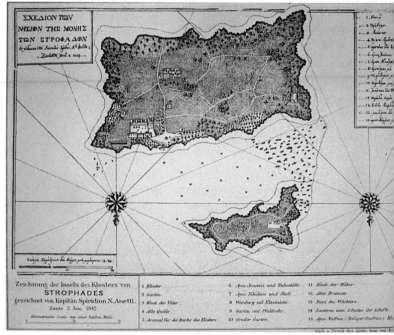

Approaching the monastery landing-place.

The two small islands, Arpina and Stamvanio, lie 44 kilometres west of the cape Kounelo of Messinia on the Peloponnese. Geologists believe these two small islands are the peaks of a mountain formed during the Quarternary period, in the Ionian sea. Its limestone strata give rise to the many natural springs on the islands.

The French writer and traveller Saint Saveur (1790) was very impressed by the fortified monastery and wrote the following descriptive piece:
" *Lying 50 paces from the sea, it consists of a tower 60 feet high and 82 feet wide, built of hewn stone on 4 levels. On the second and third level are the church and some monastic cells. The other two were designed as the living quarters of the monks. On the terrace they have set up four small canons. It is here too, that they bring up the monastery's wheat with a system of pulleys, to dry out in the sun. The wheat is then allowed to pour into the store room through a hole cut in the terrace.*

In front of the tower is an independent one storey building 150 feet wide. On the one side are the guest rooms and on the other, the dining room and monks' communal living area.

The south side of the monastery tower.

Monks from the monastery, from Salvator's book about Zakynthos (1900).

A wall surrounds the whole group of buildings, with the distance between the two buildings being 30 feet. Behind the wall's gate, which is fortified with iron plates, is a moving bridge which leads up to a lodge, where two monks of the guard live. From this lodge rises a stone stairway leading to another fortified door, which takes one into the church and the monks' cells. There is an opening above the door from which they can throw stones and other objects from the inside, at invaders trying to force the outside gate. On each side of the guest house are two watch points from where the monks keep watch over the seashore. A bell hanging next to the flag pole is sounded to warn of approaching ships.

About forty monks lived at the Monastery. They farmed the land, fished and maintained the buildings. No female was allowed to step ashore the island, and not even female animals were permitted".

Sailing towards the Strofades on a caique, one first encounters the smaller of the two, **Stamvanio**, an uninhabited island used to breed pheasants.

On the pier of the larger island, **Arpina**, one comes across the old stone fountain of the spring of St Dionysios. The top of the island is dominated by the 13th century Byzantine monastery of St Dionysios. To this monastic empire of the Strofades, came the 20 year old Dranganinos Sigouros to serve as a monk. An offspring of one of the artistocratic families of Zakynthos, he was to become the patron saint of the island, St Dionysios, as they call him on Zakynthos.

The cedar beside the well, with the Monastery in the background.

In front of monastery stands an enormous rectangular tower 26 metres high.

The monastery's entrance, next to the tower, has a fortified gate flanked by two canons and faces west. The gate opens into a beautiful yard with a picturesque well and stone stairs leading down to the monastery's cellar and up to the five floors of the tower. The stairs give out onto the roof of the monastery, which is a paved terrace.

The empty tomb of St Dionysios is on the ground floor in the chapel of St George. The remains of the saint are to be found on Zakynthos.

On the first floor of the tower is a church known as the Church of the Transfiguration or Our Lady of Everlasting Joy, which contains a marble altar screen and old icons, including the very large one of the Virgin Mary.

On the northern tip of the island stands a lighthouse, the agelesse guide of sailors.

In a small cypress wood, beneath a large white cross in the chasm of a rock is the cave of St Dionysios. Here, two monks escaping from the Turks in 1717 hid the corpse of the saint who had died in 1622. Despite the saint's wishes to be entombed in the monastery the corpse was taken to Zakynthos.

The Strofades lie in the flight-path of migrating birds, such as turtle-doves and quails, which makes them an excellent seasonal hunting ground. The islands can be reached by caique from Lagana on Zakynthos.

Index

155

BIBLIOGRAPHY

ΑΡΓΥΡΙΑΔΟΥ ΜΑΡΙΑ:
Ζάκυνθος, όπως την είδα και τη φωτογράφησα, Αθήνα 1976.
ΒΑΓΙΑΚΑΚΟΥ Δ.:
Σχέσεις Ζακύνθου και Μάνης «Αιξωνή» τ. Γ' 1953, σ.123-127
ΒΑΡΒΙΑΝΗ Ν.Α.:
Η Ζάκυνθος. Αθήνα 1977 (Εθν. Τυπογραφείο).
ΒΟΚΟΤΟΠΟΥΛΟΣ Π.:
«Ζάκυνθος» Αρχ. Δελτίο 24 (1969) Β2, σελ. 289-290
ΖΗΒΑΣ Α. ΔΙΟΝΥΣ.:
Η αρχιτεκτονική της Ζακύνθου, Αθήνα 1970.
ΖΗΒΑΣ Α. ΔΙΟΝΥΣ.:
Οι Καλύβες της Ζακύνθου, (ανάτυπο τεχν. χρον. 1970). Αθήνα 1970
ΖΩΗΣ ΛΕΩΝΙΔΑΣ:
Ιστορία της Ζακύνθου, Αθήνα 1955
ΖΩΗΣ ΛΕΩΝΙΔΑΣ:
Λεξικόν ιστορικόν και λαογραφικόν Ζακύνθου, Αθήνα (1970), 1898
ΖΩΗΣ ΛΕΩΝΙΔΑΣ:
Κρήτες εν Ζακύνθω «Επετηρίς Εταιρ. Κρητικών Σπουδών», τ.2 (1939) σ. 125.
ΖΩΗΣ ΛΕΩΝΙΔΑΣ:
Ιστορικές σελίδες Ζακύνθου, Αι εν Ζακύνθω Συντεχνίαι, Ζάκυνθος 1893
ΚΑΙΡΟΦΥΛΑ Κ.:
Η Επτάνησος υπό τους Βενετούς, Αθήνα 1942
ΚΟΝΟΜΟΥ ΝΤΙΝΟΥ:
Τσή Ζάκυθος, Αθήνα 1983
ΚΟΝΟΜΟΥ ΝΤΙΝΟΥ:
Ναοί και Μονές στη Ζάκυνθο, Αθήνα 1964
ΚΟΝΟΜΟΥ ΝΤΙΝΟΥ:
Άγιος Διονύσιος, ο πολιούχος Ζακύνθου, Αθήνα 1969
ΚΟΝΟΜΟΥ ΝΤΙΝΟΥ:
Το Ζακυνθινό λαϊκό θέατρο, «Επτανησιακά Φύλλα», Δεκ. 1953, σ. 47-48
LIVANTHINOS A.N.:
"Le climat de Zante" Annales de l'Obsevuatoire Nationale d'Athènes
XI(1930-1931) 161
ΜΥΛΩΝΑΣ ΣΠΥΡΟΣ:
Ζάκυνθος, Καλλιτεχνικός Τουριστικός Οδηγός, Αθήνα 1963
ΞΗΡΟΥΧΑΚΗΣ ΑΓΑΘΑΓΓΕΛΟΣ:
Η Βενετοκρατούμενη Ανατολή, Κρήτη και Επτάνησος, Αθήνα 1934
«ΠΕΡΙΠΛΟΥΣ»:
Ζακυνθινό, τριμηνιαίο περιοδικό για τα γράμματα και τις τέχνες, από το 1984, εκδ. Δ. Βίτσος
ΠΡΟΒΑΤΑΚΗΣ Μ. ΘΕΟΧΑΡΗΣ:
Η Αγία Μαύρα, Αθήνα 1985
ΡΩΜΑΣ ΔΙΟΝ.:
Περίπλους 1570-1870, Αθήνα 1968
ΡΩΜΑΣ ΔΙΟΝ.:
Η πόλη της Ζακύνθου πριν και μετά την ένωση «Χρονικά Ζακύθου» Α',
1964 σ. 153-175
SALVATOR LUDWING:
Zante, 2 τόμοι, Prag 1904
ΣΙΜΟΠΟΥΛΟΣ ΚΥΡ.:
Ξένοι ταξιδιώτες στην Ελλάδα, τ. Α,Β,Γ Αθήνα 1981
ΣΟΡΔΙΝΑΣ Α.:
«Λίθινα εργαλεία από την προϊστορική Ζάκυνθο», Κερκυραϊκά Χρονικά
15 (1970), σελ. 122-130

222 Recipes the GREEK Cookery Book

local specialities - festival dishes   150 colour illustrations

TOUBI'S

You can visit culinary Greece through our last edition "THE GREEK COOKERY BOOK" that we prepared for you. In this book, you will find the representative greek dishes, traditional recipes and specialities for the official holidays with easy instructions to prepare them as well as numerous and rich illustrations and also the caloris corresponding to each dish.